Reflections and Reminiscences of Police Officers

About the Editor

Sankar Sen, former Director General, National Human Rights Commission, New Delhi and former Director of the National Police Academy, Hyderabad, joined the Indian Police Service in 1960. He graduated from Presidency College, Calcutta, and obtained Master's degree in History from Calcutta University and LLB from Utkal University. He was allotted to Orissa cadre and held a number of posts with distinction. He joined the Border Security Force as the Inspector General in 1987 and was later on promoted as the Additional Director General. Thereafter, he was posted as the Director of the SVP National Police Academy (NPA), the premier institution for training of senior police officers in the country.

He was awarded the Police Medal for meritorious service in 1979 and President's Police Medal for distinguished service in 1986. On completion of his assignment in the NPA, he joined as the Director General of the National Human Rights Commission and later on functioned as the Special Rapporteur, in charge of custodial justice programmes of the NHRC. He has to his credit many books, including *Police Today and Human Rights in a Developing Society, Tryst with Law Enforcement and Human Rights; Law Enforcement and Cross Border Terrorism; Human Rights and Law Enforcement*, etc. At present, he is a Senior Fellow in the Institute of Social Sciences, New Delhi.

REFLECTIONS AND REMINISCENCES OF POLICE OFFICERS

Edited by

SANKAR SEN

CONCEPT PUBLISHING COMPANY, NEW DELHI-110059

Cataloging in Publication Data—DK
Courtesy: D.K. Agencies (P) Ltd. <docinfo@dkagencies.com>

Reflections and reminiscences of police officers / edited by Sankar Sen.

p. cm.
Contributed articles.
Includes bibliographical references.
Includes index.
ISBN 8180692361

1. Police—India—Anecdotes. I. Sen, Sankar, 1936-

DDC 363.209 2 21

ISBN 81-8069-236-1

First Published 2006

Published and Printed by
Ashok Kumar Mittal
Concept Publishing Company,
A/15-16, Commercial Block, Mohan Garden,
New Delhi-110059 (INDIA)

Phones : 25351460, 25351794
Fax : 091-11-25357103
Email : publishing@conceptpub.com

Preface

Policing is a difficult and very often a thankless job. Indeed, from no other profession so much is expected and demanded with so little recompense. But at the same time, the police function as the bulwarks of society against the forces of chaos and disruption. It is the most visible symbol of the authority of the government, and people often judge the government by the manner in which the police function. Unfortunately, because of high visibility, the lapses of the police are highlighted and achievements go unheralded. In developing countries like India, the problems of the police are further compounded by conflicting pulls and pressures and its alienation from the community due to a variety of reasons and circumstances. However, the undisputed fact remains that in India, after independence the police officers, and particularly, the police leaders, have rendered yeoman's service in holding the country together against the onslaught of the forces of disruption and secession. A number of them have laid down their lives for the cause of the nation. One feels like quoting the words of the famous Roman soldier Horatius, who stood alone on the bridge across the river Tiber against the Tuscan army:

"To every man upon the earth
Death cometh soon or late
And how can man die better
Than facing fearful odds".

However, the task of law enforcement is beset with problems and challenges. A police officer, in discharge of his duties, has to face many unforeseen and perilous situations. He often walks on a razor's edge. Even in discharge of his normal duties, he has to display tact, good humour and presence of mind of a high order. Some error of judgement at critical junctures may land him in a sea of trouble. He has also to learn and gain from the experience of others. Keeping this in mind, I requested some senior and distinguished police officers, who had served the country gallantly in various capacities, to share some of their rich and variegated experiences with the serving officers of today so that the lessons of the past are not lost for the present and coming generations of police officers. This kind of a compilation will provide them light and guidance in their professional work.

There was very good response. I received 18 contributions and many replied to me pleading inability to contribute on grounds of ill health and other constraints. Many also expressed the needless apprehension that their writings may trigger off avoidable controversies.

We are passing through a turbulent phase in country's history. Politicisation is eating into the vitals of police administration and professionalism. It is hoped that the book containing valuable experience and insightful observations of the distinguished police officers will encourage officers in the field to adhere to correct norms and rules and follow the narrow straight path. By this, they can obtain professional success, win laurels, achieve personal satisfaction and fulfilment, and also earn respect of the community.

New Delhi — Sankar Sen

Contents

Notes on Contributors

Ashwini Kumar—Ashwini Kumar is one of the most distinguished and well-decorated police officers of the country. He was Inspector General of Punjab for a number of years and retired as the Director General of the Border Security Force in January, 1979. He was the Vice President of International Olympic Committee for four years and member of the Executive Committee Board from 1980 onwards. He was awarded President's Medal for Gallantry, President's Medal for Distinguished Services and President's Medal for Meritorious Service. He was awarded Padma Bhushan for his outstanding service during the Indo-Pak War. He was adjudged the Policeman of the Millennium in Sydney for his work in security during the Olympic games. In 1997, he was awarded Medal of Merit on behalf of National Association of Olympic Committee of the World. For his outstanding work in International sports, he was awarded the rare "Olympic Order" in 2002, in Mexico.

Arun Prosad Mukherjee—Arun Prosad Mukherjee joined the Indian Police Service in 1956. He was allotted to West Bengal cadre and held many important posts in the state with great distinction. He was a senior faculty member of the National Police Academy, Mount Abu. He functioned as the Director General of Police, West Bengal till his retirement on 1st January, 1992. He was awarded Police Medal for Meritorious Service and President's Police Medal for Distinguished Service. He had worked in the CBI as Additional Director and later on as Director. He was Special Secretary to the Ministry of Home Affairs, Government of India. He was Vigilance Commissioner of West Bengal and functioned as Adviser to the Union Home

Minister. He was appointed as the Governor of Mizoram in January, 1998, and continued till 30th April 1998, when he resigned and demitted office. He is associated with various NGOs dealing with police, criminal justice and electoral reforms, tribal welfare, environment protection, etc.

A.K. Dave—A.K. Dave served in the Indian Police for 30 years from 1942 to 1972 and held many important posts with great distinction. He was deputed to the Government of India in 1953 as an adviser to the Neutral Nations Repatriation Commission, a UN body engaged in facilitating exchange of PsOW of North Korea, South Korea and China. He served the Intelligence Bureau for 18 years and held the post of Joint Director IB. He retired from IB prematurely and moved into hotel planning, constructions, commissioning of hotels and tourism studies for the next 28 years. He was the first CEO of Welcome Group of Hotels of ITC. He also headed the public sector India Tourism Development Corporation and the Ashok Group of Hotels as the Chairman and Managing Director. Later, from 1981 to 1989, he was an independent Hotels and Tourism Consultant for nearly 100 hotels and tourism projects. He was also the President of Retired Senior Police Service Officers' Association and kept his interest till the end in national and international security affairs. He expired on 16th November, 2004.

S.V.M. Tripathy—S.V.M. Tripathy joined IPS in 1961 (UP cadre) after a three years stint as an Assistant Professor in Gorakhpur University. He served as Senior Superintendent of Police in a number of districts in UP, besides holding important staff assignments. He became the Director General of Police in UP in 1992. He was also the Director General of CRPF from where he retired on 30th June, 1996. He also served as a Special Rapporteur of the National Human Rights Commission. At present, he is a Member of UP Human Rights Commission and also a Member of the Executive Council of Gorakhpur University. He contributes articles for professional journals and is on the guest faculty of a number of training institutions.

Prakash Singh—Prakash Singh is a distinguished police officer, who served in the turbulent areas of Punjab, UP, Assam, Nagaland and Jammu & Kashmir. He was the Director General of Border Security Force and Police Chief of Uttar Pradesh and Assam. The Government of India in recognition of his contribution in the field of law enforcement and national security awarded him Padma Shri in 1991. A well-known writer, Singh has written books titled, *'Nagaland'*, *'Naxalite Movement in India'* (translated in French also), *'Disaster Response in India'* and *'Kohima to Kashmir'*. He is an authority on international terrorism and has given talks on the subject at different fora in different countries, particularly, in the USA.

B. J. Misar—He joined the Indian Police Service in 1958 and retired in the rank of the Director General of Police. He held with distinction important posts like the Commissioner of Police, Pune, Special Inspector General of Police, CID, Maharashtra, Principal Secretary, Home Department, Government of Maharashtra. He was awarded the Indian Police Medal for Meritorious Service (1975) and President's Police Medal for Distinguished Service (1986). He has authored a number of insightful books, namely, *'Human Rights and Law Enforcement'*, *'Human Rights the Only Key to Police Success'*, *'Encounters and the Law'*, *Directive Principles of Crime Prevention'*, and *'Prosecutor's Digest'*. After retirement, he has been associated with a number of social and cultural organisations. He is also the Executive Member of Maharashtra Police Research Centre, Pune.

B.R. Kalyanpurkar—B.R. Kalyanpurkar joined the Indian Police Service in 1950 and was allotted to the former Bombay cadre. He served in three districts, now in Maharashtra and later on in three districts now in Gujarat. He was then selected for deputation to the Government of India. He spent 26 years doing external and internal intelligence work, before being posted as the Director General, Bureau of Police Research and Development. After retiring from service, he enrolled himself as an advocate and did Legal Aid work at the Supreme Court for 10 years. He is now settled in Mysore.

D.K. Arya—D.K. Arya joined the Indian Police Service in 1960 and was allotted to Madhya Pradesh cadre. After initial years in Madhya Pradesh, he served in the Indo Tibetan Border Police Force (ITBP) on deputation. He held the post of the Director of the Border Security Force (BSF) Training Academy at Tikampur. He later on became the Director General of Police, Madhya Pradesh. He served as the Director General of ITBP and Director General of BSF. He was Adviser to the Governor of UP. He underwent the prestigious International Humanitarian Law course from San Remo, Italy, and Human Rights courses from Geneva and Bangkok. He now assists ICRC in its dissemination activities in India and abroad. He is a keen golfer, closely associated with mountaineering, water sports, canoeing, adventure promotion, environment protection and peace and unity movement in South Asia.

B.S. Das—After serving in UP in various assignments till 1960, he joined the Ministry of External Affairs in 1961, where he served till 1974. He held important assignments in Ministry, USSR, London, Bhutan and Sikkim. He was the first Ambassador of India to Bhutan from 1968-1972. He served as the Chief Executive in Sikkim during the troubled times from 1973-1974. Afterwards, he joined the Public Sector and served as the Chairman, International Airport Authority of India till 1979. Thereafter, he was posted as the Chairman-cum-M.D., Air India till 1981. On retirement, Sri Das joined the private sector and now heads two companies as Chairman. He was awarded Padma Shri in 1972, and remains associated with the Institute of Asian Studies, Osmania University, Jaipur University, and the Institute of Chinese Studies, University of Delhi. Shri Das was also a Visiting Professor at the School of International Studies at the Jawaharlal Nehru University.

P.S. Ramamohan Rao—P.S. Ramamohan Rao joined the Indian Police Service in 1956 and held many posts in his state cadre in Andhra Pradesh and in Government of India with great distinction. He served very successfully in the Intelligence Bureau for a long spell and had a stint in the Railway Protection Force. He was Director General of Police, Andhra Pradesh and

Chairman, Hyderabad Allwyn. He was Governor of Tamil Nadu from January 2002 to November 2004.

D.C. Nath—D.C. Nath – a 1960 batch IPS officer of West Bengal cadre, a former Special Director, Intelligence Bureau, Government of India, is currently the Executive President & CEO of the International Institute of Security & Safety Management (IISSM). He served on deputation to the Gore Committee on Police Training (1972). He has been a regular contributor of valuable papers and articles to All India Police Science Congress for long and was the recipient of the Prime Ministers' Silver Cup in Essay Competition for two successive years in 1980 and 1981. He is a recipient of the Indian Police Medal for Meritorious Service (1976) and Presidents' Police Medal for Distinguished Service (1987). He has recently authored a highly acclaimed book on *'Intelligence Imperatives for India'*, an insightful publication on security threats and assessments from varied angles.

Kalyan Kumar Mitra—Kalyan Kumar Mitra, took Master's degree in Economics from Kolkata University and joined the IPS in 1960. Having spent early years of his service in Orissa, he joined RAW in the Cabinet Secretariat. He was the Director, Aviation Research Centre of the Government of India and retired as the Principal Director of the Directorate General Security set-up in 1995. He was a member of the committee appointed by the Government of India to restructure the SSB, a paramilitary force under the Ministry of Home Affairs. He contributes articles in journals and dailies and is currently associated with several organisations dealing with national security and strategic thinking.

Ved Marwah—A distinguished member of the Indian Police Service, Shri Ved Marwah has served in many states and held many important posts. He was a member of the first National Security Advisory Board, Convenor of the Internal Security Group of the Board, Adviser to the Governor of Jammu and Kashmir, Adviser to the Governor of Bihar, Special Secretary, Internal Security, Ministry of Home Affairs, Director General, National

Security Guards, Commissioner of Police, Delhi, IGP, Mizoram and First Secretary, High Commission of India, London. He is the author of the book "Uncivil Wars: Pathology of Terrorism in India". The awards he has received include: Padmashri, President's Police Medal for Gallantry, President's Medal for Distinguished Services and President's Police Medal for Meritorious Service. He has served as the Governor of Mizoram and Manipur. Currently, he is the Governor of Jharkhand. A post-graduate from St. Stephen's College, Delhi, he received a diploma in Public Administration from the University of Manchester.

Chaman Lal—Chaman Lal is an officer of the Indian Police Service of 1964 batch. Besides holding important posts in different ranks in his parent cadre Madhya Pradesh, he served on deputation to the BSF, ITBP, Shah Commission of Enquiry, SPG, Punjab and Nagaland Police. In Punjab, he was the IGP, incharge of operation Black Thunder, which is acknowledged as one of the most successful operations of the police against the militants. He served as DGP Nagaland and retired as Additional DG BSF on 30th September, 1996. Since 1997, he is working for the NHRC in the field of prison, mental health, child labour, bonded labour, etc. He is a recipient of the Police Medal for Meritorious Service and President's Police Medal for Distinguished Service. He was awarded *Padmashree* for his commendable work in the Punjab.

F.T.R. Colaso—F.T.R. Colaso joined the Indian Police Service in 1961. Before joining the Police service he worked as a lecturer in economics at St. Joseph's College in Bangalore. He held with great distinction a number of important assignments in Karnataka police. In 1986, he was specially selected and sent on promotion as DGP Jammu and Kashmir. On completion of his assignment there, he was posted in the BSF, where he worked as Inspector General in the North-East and also at BSF Headquarters in New Delhi. He was awarded the President's Police Medal for Distinguished Service in 1989. On his reversion to his parent cadre, he was posted as the Director General of Police, Karnataka state. After his retirement, he has remained closely associated with several associations and organisations involved in social and community service.

R. Ramalingam—R. Ramalingam joined the Indian Police Service in 1960, and was allotted to Karnataka cadre. He held with great distinction many important posts. He was the chief of the Railway Protection Force (RPF) in Southern Railways from 1982-89. He was the Commissioner of Police, Bangalore and Director General of Police, Karnataka. He was awarded the Police Medal for Meritorious Service as well as the President's Police medal for Distinguished Service.

E. Rammohan—E. Rammohan joined the Indian Police Service in 1965 and was allotted to Assam cadre. He served in various capacities in paramilitary forces like the Indo Tibetan Border Police, the Central Reserve Police Force, the Border Security Force. He has had first hand experience of heading counter-insurgency operations in Northeast and Kashmir. He was the Inspector General of the Central Reserve Police Force in the Northeast in 1993 and Inspector General of the Border Security Force in Kashmir from 1993 to 1995. He retired as the Director General of the Border Security Force after heading the force successfully for three years. After retirement, he functioned as the adviser to the Governor of Manipur during 2001-2002.

S.K. Sharma—Born in 1933, S.K. Sharma is B.Sc. and LL.B. from Delhi University and MA (Public Administration) from Punjab University. He practiced Law in Delhi before joining the IPS in 1958. He was allotted to Rajasthan cadre where he held charge of four Districts as the Superintendent of Police and three Ranges as Dy. Inspector General of Police. He served in the Central Government on deputation in senior positions in the Border Security Force, LBS National Academy of Administration, Mussoorie, Shah Commission of Inquiry, ITDC and Central Industrial Security Force. He was the first Director General of the National Crime Records Bureau. He had been the first IPS officer to be trained in computers in 1968 to develop computer-based systems for the Indian police.

Post retirement, he was adviser, Computer Maintenance Corporation (CMC), then a Government of India Undertaking, visiting expert in UNAFEI, a UN Institute in Tokyo, Executive President and CEO, Indian Institute of Security and Safety Management, and Consultant Jardine Securicor, Hong Kong.

1

Mukerian Dacoity Case

ASHWINI KUMAR

It was a black, windy night – the inky darkness around was pregnant with an atmosphere breathing of sanguinary crime or perhaps, something worse. As a railway official on duty, that night, remarked, "there appeared to be some evil in the wind". This was the night of the Mukerian dacoity – the night between the 1st and 2nd April, 1956 – when a crime so heinous in its concept and execution was committed – that it had no parallel in Northern India.

That very night eight desperate looking men, boarded a train for Mukerian, a small town in district Hoshiarpur, Punjab at about two or three hours before midnight in small separate groups. This train plied in the Punjab, between Jullundur and towns of Tanda, Dasyua, Mukerian and Pathankot, and ran almost along the river Beas. Three of these desperadoes, Gian Singh, Faqir Singh and Surinder Singh, got into the train at a way side station at Cholong, nearer Jullundur than Mukerian, and another five came from the Jullundur side with the gang leader, who at that moment had not been identified amongst them by name, on strict instruction from another accomplice, who appeared to be the most weathered and experienced rough-neck. The entire gang consisted of – 1. Gian Singh, 2. Faqir Singh, 3. Surinder Singh, 4. Jagjit Singh Kairon, 5. Rur Singh, 6. Gurcharan Singh, 7. Mohan Singh, and 8. Moola. The leader, as it turned out later, was Jagjit Singh of village Kairon in district Amritsar and was a nephew of the well-known Chief Minister Pratap Singh Kairon of Punjab. The one, who looked more experienced than the others, had a mole on his face and was fair, and had recently undergone some years of imprisonment in the Amritsar jail, for serious criminal offences. His companion in jail had been Faqiria, one of the eight desperadoes in the train. They were heavy and stockily built, with picturesque tall exteriors, proportionate to their breadth of shoulder and depth of chest. Some of them could have passed off as middle aged, but looked youthful enough, though the contours of their faces were firmly etched, by what must have been toil, hardship and even harder drink. They were a silent group, whispering amongst themselves, exhibiting a furtiveness, which gave the whole compartment an eerie look. Most of them were without tickets. Moola, one of the "toughs", had brought them to an earlier station to escape any subsequent detection. They all looked as if they were proof against any crisis, most of them were square jawed, displaying a rugged pertinacity and indomitability, which is an outstanding characteristic of the Majha Sikhs (Sikhs belonging to the erstwhile Lahore and Amritsar district). They appeared that dark night as typical hoodlums, with their jutting jaws and a swagger to their shoulders, as if saying that they were not too mindful of the police and were like crazy bootleggers, or smugglers or cut throats, who constantly exhibit brute force, as a virtue.

Punjab with such volatile elements had never been a peaceful haven for saints. The soil was rich, and water was never scarce. With not too great an effort, crops were grown in abundance. Springs and summers were always emerald green and its winters were warm and sunny, and thousands of trees provided shade in the hot season. The countryside was teeming with residents, who appeared to be full of vigour, with music and dance in their veins. They were always exquisitely happy. But here and there, on the periphery of this peaceful group, were desperate men, who lived a life of drink and degradation, and were ready to eke out their livelihood by crime, mayhem and murder. These interlopers never lived within the law, and were devoid of honour and virtue. One could only loathe them. They had all the vices but no virtues of some of the lordly Jat

Sikhs, their forbears. It was not possible for them to be anything like the peaceful, but sensitive Sikh Jat tribes of the Majha – who were proud and patriotic, and simple in their manners – but sensitive to insult, and would go to any length to avenge a slur on their honour and fair name. By both fire and sword, the Sikh Maharaja Ranjit Singh had subjugated the entire rebellious tract between Afghanistan and the Sutluj river (Punjab) in the beginning of the nineteenth century, but could not give them a sense of unity and left behind only traditions of valour, hospitality and courage, amongst his populace.

Four of the eight dacoits were Jat Sikhs, the fifth was a Labana Sikh and three were village Sikh "Suniars" – known for rascality and low virtue. Two of them had been recently released from Amritsar jail (Moola and Faqira) and had done time for crime against person and property. Three of the experienced felons had already done a reconnaissance a few days earlier of neighbouring towns on this isolated railway tract between Jullundur and Pathankot (in the foothills of the Himalayas) of small townships like Dasyua Tanda and Mukerian, which had small well known nationalised banks, but which were lightly guarded.[1] There were no military screening posts, except after the Mukerian town. Telephone wires were erected overhead and could easily be disrupted. Their goal was to loot a bank, after disabling the small police station staff responsible for law and order in that area, by killing and injuring personnel, and damaging its firearms that could be used against them and then disappear with the cash and booty, before sunrise, not towards Pathankot because of the Army pickets *en route*, but towards Jullundur. The "get away" vehicle was to be picked up from one of the many transport depots along this route. The local population or police, if interfered, was to be shot, and a spell of terror was to be spread, if necessary.

Faqir Singh, Moola and Gian Singh finally chose Mukerian, because of the easy approach to the police building from the railway station, and also of close proximity of the bus depot to the Punjab National Bank, which they wanted to rifle. They were to be well armed with safe breaking implements, torches, hammers and lethal weapons.

On the fateful night, they had collected from various small stations between Jullundur and Mukerian, into a compartment, which had the 'senior' Moola in it, and who openly displayed himself in the compartment, so as to attract the other gang members, where he was sitting. All eight of them detrained at Mukerian at about 9 PM (1st of April) on the "off side" of the station, alongwith a small box and a bed roll. Two of them went away to a nearby field to unroll the bedding, and procure from it and the box, weapons, hammers, jennies and torches which they needed to aggress and force open doors and safes. Between 9 PM and mid-night, they cut the overhead wires of telephones and those of railway signalling. They further procured a wooden 'harvesting' contraption, from the surrounding fields, which they could use to scale the rear wall of the police station.

On reaching the police station, seven of them scaled its rear wall and got on to its roof, and the last one knocked at the main gate which was closed, and spoke to the armed sentry through the door, who was inside the police station building. Whilst a conversation started with the sentry, three of the dacoits, climbed down into the police station inner compound, overpowered the sentry, who was talking to their companion. Moola, one of the criminals, snatched away the sentry's rifle and climbed on to the roof again to keep guard. The Sub-Inspector incharge of the police station was away with a local search party to trace a missing child. The Head Constable, who was the senior officer present, was aroused from his sleep by the noise that was going on, and grappled with Rur Singh, one of the intruding dacoits and felled him. Head Constable Nirbhai Singh, true to his name, acted fearlessly, but was shot dead by dacoits Jagjit Singh Kairon and Gurcharan Singh. The remaining five or six policemen, who were present and had been woken up, were shepherded into a barrack and locked up. The keys of the Malkhana, which were in the custody of the deceased H.C. Nirbhai Singh, were obtained from his bed, and some of the arms which were lying there insecure were lifted away. The service rifles, which were locked in a rack, could not be procured, because the key of the rack got broken when the dacoits tried to open it.

The following arms and objects were taken away:

1. One rifle
2. Two D.B.B.L. guns
3. Three revolvers
4. A pistol
5. Bandoliers and ammunition
6. A signet ring
7. A wristwatch of a constable

(All these articles were fortunately identifiable)

An iron safe, which was embedded in the floor, was also looted and more than Rs. 1,600 belonging to the postal department taken away. There was also one prisoner in the lock-up, who was freed by them, but who out of fear, refused to accept his liberation ! Seven of the dacoits left the police station by the front gate, but one of them remained behind to shut the main gate from inside, and then joined the others by coming down from the roof, via the wooden frame, which had been planted in the rear.

On emerging from the police station after having killed the officer incharge, H.C. Nirbhai Singh, at about 2.00 AM on the morning of 2nd April, 1956, they made their way towards the Punjab National Bank, which was situated only a furlong away in a residential street. They forced open its outer shuttered door, and pounced on the chowkidar who was asleep, with a gun by his side. In no time, before the chowkidar could resist, they shot him through the abdomen. Later (on the next day), he died of his wounds. They ransacked the bank, opened a safe and filing cabinets, but were disgusted and disappointed to find no cash in them. In the meantime, from a house opposite the bank, someone switched on a light. One of the dacoits fired towards the light a number of times, till it was switched off, leaving the area in the dark again, but the occupants were now fully aware of what was afoot in the bank – a dacoity by eight people, who were also cursing their luck, at having drawn a blank to rifle the banks safe. During the night, whilst they were moving from the police station to the bank and the bus stand, they were accosted by a couple of persons. They were loudly cursing, possibly, at the poor turn of events, in not having obtained any money from the bank. The eight dacoits now, at the goading of their leader, decided to quit the scene. They had by now heard gunshots and police whistle blasts not far away from where they were. They quickly made their way to the town's bus stand, which was about 400 yards away. On reaching the stand, they aroused a driver and forced him to drive them towards Jullundur. After a short distance, they pushed the driver out of the vehicle, and Jagjit Singh Kairon, the leader, took over the wheel but nearly crashed into two wayside trucks, which were standing on the road.

At about 3.45 a.m., I was aroused (I was D.I.G. Jullundur Range, living in Jullundur Cantt.) from my sleep by a phone call from the Post Master of Mukerian, that the local police station had been attacked by a gang of eight dacoits, who had fled Mukerian in a passenger lorry towards Jullundur, after ransacking the Punjab National Bank, shooting its chowkidar down. The Officer Incharge of the police station had also been shot and the premises had been ransacked. I called back, on the military line (the civilians line apparently had been tampered with) and the Post Master again related the horrid story of the police station having been looted, arms taken away, and the local bank ransacked. The gang of eight dacoits had fled towards Jullundur.

As there was no time to be lost, I rang up the Superintendent of Police (Jullundur) and asked him to send the gist of the information I had received to all District and State Headquarters and further send his two armed reserves to Mukerian, along the Pathankot highway, and apprehend if possible, the dacoits alongwith the getaway vehicle. I also gave instructions to the SPs of Amritsar, Jullundur, Gurdaspur and Kangra, to make themselves available at Mukerian by 9.00 AM. After a few minutes, I, alongwith a rifleman available in my Bungalow, and my armed driver-constable, drove towards Mukerian hoping to corner the vehicle on the forty-five mile tract between Jullundur and Mukerian. At the 11th mile from Jullundur towards Mukerian, I spotted a bus parked on the side of the main road. I got down from my car quickly opened the bonnet of the vehicle, and found the engine hot, and presumed that it had been just switched off. In my mind I concluded that it was most probably the 'get-away' vehicle. A few hundred yards away to the right (it was still dark), I saw the lights of a stationery train whistling *en route* to Jullundur. Thinking that the dacoits may be attempting to 'sneak' away in a train, I ran across the fields, which lay between the road and the train, but saw the train steam away before I could reach the station. The Station Master, however, informed me that no one had alighted or caught the train from this railway station —Dhogharri. I ran back to the main road to my car, and sped towards Mukerian, little knowing that due to a dispute between the gang members (this was learnt later), who were hiding in the dark, in the thick foliage along the road, where the bus was parked, my fate was being decided amongst them. It appears that one of the accused, Moola, wanted me to be killed whilst I was running towards the stationery train at Dhogharri. Jagjit Singh Kairon did not agree, as he felt that the police, which had obviously been alerted, would learn from the new slaying that the criminals had got off the vehicle there, and taken to another road which lay a few yards away, and joined this spot to the Grand Trunk Road between Jullundur and Amritsar, and which could lead to their apprehension. Most of the ruffians belonged to Amritsar district.

I arrived in Mukerian at about 6.00 a.m. and proceeded to the police station. The huge crowd collected just outside the precincts of the police station was a wailing sorry lot. Inside the police station, on the floor of the courtyard, lay the body of the courageous Head Constable Nirbhai Singh, who had resisted and felled one of the miscreants. His face, martial in demeanour, was already covered by flies and ants (as no one had been allowed to touch it). Silently crying were the near relatives, in a corner of the courtyard. It was a gory sight, with anguished policemen, completely rudderless, and remorse and guilt written all over their faces. I took immediate steps to fence the various points through which the miscreants had made entry into the police building, and on which footprints and fingerprints had been left. Instructions were given for summoning the state's ace operatives in scientific aids to investigation – fingerprint experts, photographers and medico-legal experts to the site. All the objects both in the Bank, police station and the 'get away vehicle' on which any evidence had been left were to be closely examined, photographed and the clues preserved.

The F.I.R., which ultimately plays a key part in the investigation of the case, had been registered under Section 396/397 IPC, and had already been carefully written out by the Station House Officer, bringing out clearly the arms that had been stolen and the objects that had been tampered with. The informant was the constable on duty, and very strict instructions were given for obtaining all help from the residents of Mukerian.

I immediately addressed the very large gathering of citizens, and assured them that the dacoits would be apprehended as quickly as possible – but not without their help. The police force would give unstinted help to clear all hurdles. I vowed that no stone would be left unturned to bring to book the perpetrators of this dastardly crime. I reminded them that a swift and successful conclusion of the case would be possible only if every resident in and around Mukerian would render help by way of information about the miscreants.

A couple of hours later, the Senior SPs of all the surrounding districts reached Mukerian. After a detailed inspection we came to the conclusion that:

1. It was an organised crime by an experienced gang, and
2. The perpetrators could be

   (a) Hardened criminals recently released from jails in the adjoining areas,
   (b) Political workers, knowledgeable of the tactics of a highly lethal organised crime, trained in military and police tactics, and
   (c) Ordinary criminals led by an experienced bad character belonging to the police station area around Mukerian.

Accordingly, three groups, each, under a Senior SP were immediately formed and started working. They were to report to me personally twice a day. They were to strictly ensure that during interrogation of suspects, third degree methods, which often mislead investigators, were not be employed, and if used, would result in strong disciplinary action. No contact with the press or politicians was to be maintained. Any dereliction on this behalf would attract similar action against them. The press received no official report till the case had been worked out.

Time and again, my mind quickly rehearsed the vicious crime that had been committed and thought of the various criminals, who could have committed it. Ex-criminal-tribes, smugglers, recently released dacoits, politically motivated sedition-oriented cadres, and nefarious individuals with criminal connections in the neighbouring states came to my mind, as well as the Bundle 'A' criminals of the police station who are "criminal history sheeters" and regularly report their movements to the police. The finger of suspicion moved towards the last category for the simple reason that some of them had shown knowledge of the geography of Mukerian, and knew where the bus stand was, and one of them was knowledgeable enough it seemed of the manner in which one could make a quick get away in various directions. They had all shown daring in plenty and assaulted the police victims with abuse typical of "Majha territory" – "mother incestuous" – in a dialect used only in Amritsar or Lahore. They were sturdy, well built, and had obviously done their home-work – by a good recce, drawn a plan to disable the local police station, and spread terror by shooting the senior officer, or whosoever tried to resist them and then loot the bank. The manner in which they had traversed the ploughed-up fields, and crudely cut not only the telephone wires, but even signalling cables showed that they had a 'unsophisticated' background. Their brash manner knew no limits – they had no masks and made no effort to conceal their faces. There was, amongst them, a middle-aged 'tough', who was very fair and had a mole on his right cheek. They did not panic except when they were leaving and had heard police whistles blowing, and shots fired in the air. What puzzled one was as to why they left towards Jullundur?

Right from the very onset of the investigation, I told the local Superintendent of Police, an extremely honest and experienced officer S. Anup Singh – to carefully preserve all fingerprints, foot prints and every property left behind by the criminals. Investigation of a murder case is a very exacting task. There are so many factors to be kept in focus to prove a serious crime like murder in a court of law. The Mukerian dacoity was unique in all its facets. Never before in the Punjab (1956) a crime involving an attack on a police station, murder and looting of a bank had taken place. Why now? Was there any nexus between the criminals and any nascent political forces?

Justice G.D. Khosla, in a commentary on the detection of the Mukerian case, had observed:

"When the news of this daring outrage spread through the state, it caused consternation and threw the entire police force into a state of stern indignation. Such a bold and vicious assault on the guardians of law and order had never been heard of in the whole history of the Punjab administration, which had always boasted of 'strong' police service, able to deal effectively with the most turbulent and the most desperate criminals".

"Other states had always admired the Punjab Police, and their methods had aroused envy. During the days of the British Raj, Punjab policemen were often requisitioned to suppress political disturbances and the nefarious activities of revolutionary gangs, and they had invariably achieved complete success, whatever the envious ones might say about the manner in which they employed their extraordinary talents. In independent India, when Bhupat's gang of robbers and murderers was terrorising the people of Saurashtra, the Government of India had sent a Punjab policeman to deal with the situation, and he had captured or 'liquidated' the entire gang so swiftly and effectively that 'its leader, Bhupat, had been obliged to flee and seek asylum in Pakistan, whence he never returned home. Peace had been restored to Saurashtra by a Punjabi. It was this same Punjabi, Mr. Ashwini Kumar, who now held the post of Deputy Inspector-General of Police and was incharge of the Western Range in which the town of Mukerian is situated. He at once assumed personal control of the investigation and sent out instructions calling upon all police officers to strain every nerve and spare no effort to trace the culprits and bring them to book".

"There was almost an unparalleled wealth of data to proceed from. The dacoits had been seen by several persons who had had ample opportunity of observing their features. There were, to begin with, one head constable and four constables, in whose presence Nirbhai Singh was murdered and the store-room plundered. Lal Masih, the inmate of the lock-up, had also seen some of the offenders. Then there was Dr. Bal Krishan, the resident of the house opposite the bank premises. He told the police that he would be able to identify some of the culprits. The driver of the bus in which the dacoits had escaped would also be of some assistance in the matter of identification, and finally there was Daffedar Mota Singh, who claimed to have met the dacoits when they were going to the Punjab National Bank after ransacking the police station. The dacoits were obviously fearless and experienced and the Police Fingerprint Bureau at Phillaur must have records of the fingerprints of many of them. The impressions found on the steering wheel, windscreen and mudguard of the bus on the various articles in the bank room would surely enable the bureau officials to trace the culprits. Trace marks of eight different feet were observed on the soft ground at the back of the police station and also in the courtyard. These were carefully examined and moulds were prepared for them. An experienced tracker would be able unerringly to pick out corresponding tracks whenever he saw them again, and he would be able to demonstrate to the court the accuracy of his observation by making a comparison of the moulds with the feet of the culprits when they were found. Almost all the stolen articles were identifiable, because they bore individual markings, which obviate any possibility of error. The firearms had numbers engraved upon them. The watch, the ring and the gun licence also bore the names of their owners. The leather bag, too, would be recognised by Sub-Inspector Shiv Parshad."

Genesis of the Crime

Moola and Faqira had been in Amritsar jail till 15th March, 1956. During their incarceration they had conspired and made a plan to commit a daring robbery of a bank in a small town, which did not have big police presence. After release, and through their shady contacts, they organised a gang of hard drinking criminal 'Majhails' (residents of Majha) known for their ruthlessness, alongwith three goldsmiths, for the disposal of stolen goods. There was also a lower caste Labana Jat, a cut-throat refugee from Pakistan. They chose to strike at Mukerian after a preliminary reconnaissance.

We planned and spread a wide net in which hundreds of rough-necks were interrogated, but to no avail. As a matter of fact, during the initial stages two of the accused had been picked up for interrogation about their movements on that night, but had been let off. SSP Amritsar, after a few days, gave news that a prisoner by the name of Moola and his companion Faqira had been released by the Amritsar jail on 15th March, 1956, and their physical appearance corresponded with two of the accused. When Moola's house was raided he was missing and there was no way of contacting him. Faqira similarly was also missing.

Just after Baisakhi (13th, 14th) April, the case began to take life. To begin with, there was great deal of groping in the dark and floundering. The public was getting restive, and the administration became even more critical. As matters stood then, although evidence against some of the dacoits was not substantial, no court would doubt the sterling qualities of the recoveries, the fingerprints and identification.

Unfortunately, none of the dacoits could be traced through the "ten-finger system". It could only confirm identification after arrest.

I had great faith in the system of planned interrogation of a wide spectrum of bad characters, particularly of Kapurthala and Hoshiarpur. We relentlessly collected them and grilled them in an absolutely thorough manner. They did not take long to wilt. Rur Singh hopelessly entangled himself into immobility with the combined staff of Hoshiarpur, Kapurthala and Amritsar police. He was ambushed and way laid on one occasion, and stolen weapons of the police station were recovered from him. The next to fall, after Rur Singh, was Gian Singh. They returned not only valuable stolen property, but gave information about the future movements of the gang. They informed us that some of the more desperate members of the gang were contemplating a robbery at Gobindpur Mandi, and then making their way to Amritsar, for a safer haven, and then possibly slip across the border. I handled this information personally, and arrested an entire train as it arrived inside the Jullundur Railway Station, on the 18th April, 1956. The accused, as we were unaware of their identity, escaped from there by taxi, but we chased them closely into Amritsar district, where an armed detachment was lying in wait at their homes. After some very deft movements in their area, the Amritsar police and I cornered them by the morning of 19th May, 1956, and both Mohan Singh and Gurcharan Singh were liquidated. The third miscreant made a get away, but we were all the time breathing down his neck. On the afternoon of the 3rd May, I pinned him down not far from where his companions had fallen, in the heart of Amritsar district. After drilling holes in the roof of his home, where he was obstinately hiding and was not surrendering himself, he was smoked out, and came out with his gun firing so as to escape arrest. He was gunned down and liquidated.

Jagjit Singh meekly surrendered near his house in Amritsar, constantly protesting his innocence.

Thus, in a matter of few days, with the speed of a whirlwind, we had accounted for most of the gangsters.

The picture had turned round miraculously, and out of eight accused, six had been apprehended, and three liquidated. Only two, Faqir Singh and Moola, remained free and were being chased from pillar to post. They were finally traced to Pillibhit in U.P. where Moola was arrested and then brought to Punjab, and Faqira was destroyed by an informer, who had gone to fetch him.

Thus all the eight, who committed the crime, were disposed of as follows:

1.	Mohan Singh	liquidated
2.	Gurcharan Singh	
3.	Surinder/Swinder Singh	
4.	Faqira—liquidated and dead	
5.	Gian Singh was made an approver	
6.	Jagjit Singh Kairon	arrested and in prison
7.	Rur Singh	
8.	Moola of Amritsar	

The evidence against the above three was cast iron. It was felt that no court could easily acquit them.

A serious impediment to the investigation was created by then Chief Minister S. Pratap Singh Kairon of Punjab. He personally conveyed to me that his "nephew", Jagjit Singh Kairon, the apprehended leader of the eight member gang, was not to be formally charged, but to be 'brought to book' by other means as he had brought shame on the family. He even tried to muscle in his presence by contacting some of my subordinates, and I strongly resented his interference. Things came to a head, which resulted in my transfer to another Range, two years prior to the completion of my tenure. This open confrontation 'saved' the case of any further interference or tampering with the investigation of the case, which already due to the circumstances and the gravity of the case had been nearly completed.

News that the Chief Minister was trying to interfere in this case spread like wild-fire. Huge rallies took place in the entire state, with the public shouting "Chacha Chor, Bhatija Daku, Hai, Hai". The public, thus, saved the case from an unholy end.

The police lost no time in marshalling evidence against the accused and the commitment proceedings began before a Sessions Court in Hoshiarpur in early 1957. We could, with advantage, congratulate ourselves that we had successfully broken the back of a dangerous conspiracy, involving the death of a police officer, looting of a police station and a bank, which created strong feelings in the public mind that lawlessness was rife in the entire state of Punjab. This crime had important repercussions in the Punjab in later years. Eight dacoits, who had conspired to commit this crime, had all been accounted for. The arms they had stolen had been recovered. Four of the accused—Mohan Singh, Gurcharan Singh, Surinder Singh and Faqira—had been liquidated. We had enough evidence and material in our possession to bring the remaining accused to the hangman's noose. By way of abundant precaution, Gian Singh was made an approver. The remaining three—Jagjit Singh Kairon (nephew of the Chief Minister), Rur Singh and Moola—had enough evidence stacked against them to get a verdict of guilty.

1. Rur had been found in the possession of a stolen gun from the Mukerian Police station, apart from a signet ring and a licence document belonging to the SHO of Mukerian.
2. Jagjit Singh was fully incriminated by the recovery from him of the revolver with which he had shot H.C. Nirbhai Singh. His palm and fingerprints had been found on the get away vehicle.
3. Moola was nailed by the recovery from him of a stolen revolver belonging to the SHO of Mukerian, as also his fingerprints from the filing cabinet in the bank, which the dacoits had attempted to loot. Apart from all the evidence mentioned above, there was the statement of the approver against all the three, and voluminous jail and other evidence showing how some of them had been in jails together as well as their movements before and after commission of the dacoity.

The accused were committed to stand trial before the Sessions Judge S. Manohar Singh on March 25, 1957, which ended in their conviction on July 11, 1957. They were separately sentenced to be hanged for dacoity and murder, 129 witnesses appeared for the prosecution and 29 witnesses appeared for the defence. The case was referred to the High Court for confirmation. The accused also appealed against the orders of the Sessions Judge. A bench of two judges, comprising Justice

G.D. Khosla and Justice Gurnam Singh, heard their submissions.

The hearing lasted ten days. Whereas Justice G.D. Khosla had no doubt about the guilt of the accused, Justice Gurnam Singh was not fully satisfied. He disregarded the overwhelming evidence of fingerprints, recoveries and identifications. He felt that the prosecution story was 'too perfect' to be true, and further that the four accused, who had been shot, were perhaps the real perpetrators, and the rest, with the possible exception of Gian Singh, were still to be 'traced'. Jagjit Singh Kairon, Rur Singh and Moola, according to him, were innocent.

A third judge – the Chief Justice – heard the appeal himself and agreed with Justice G.D. Khosla, and the accused, despite their appeal to the Supreme Court, which was rejected, were sentenced to death and were hung in April 1958. Justice had been quick, and the accused brought to book, pitilessly.

It was a herculean task to get Jagjit Singh Kairon hung for his derring-do and strong political clout. His otherwise genial nature amongst his tough companions misled observers about his inner harsh and steely nature. Only the glitter in his dark eyes gave a clue of the hard steel out of which he had been smelted. His "uncle", the Chief Minister, I always felt, feared him, and was, therefore, 'soft' towards him. As for myself, it was ironic that after almost eight years, in 1965, I was recalled from leave, which I had obtained on my brother's death, to trace, yet again, and this time, no other than the murderer of S. Pratap Singh Kairon, who was butchered alongwith three aides, on the Grand Trunk Road, at 12.30 p.m. in the afternoon, in the presence of about 70 people. No one raised a finger against the four assailants. Sucha Singh, the leader of the gang, just walked away from the scene of this bloody crime ! I had to chase Sucha Singh to Nepal, where after capturing him, I myself was taken prisoner by the Nepalese army and had to spend more than a week, alongwith my prisoner, in a filthy jail ! Sucha Singh too, like the Mukerian murderers, was ultimately hung in Ambala jail.

Nemesis had its way, but not before S. Pratap Singh Kairon had all but ruined my police career. Why cannot people understand that we policemen are also human beings championing human rights even in jail. Being human, we do get aroused at times, by the senseless filth that criminals strew all over the field of their activity, which is full of gross self-indulgence, militant selfishness and wretched vandalism !

2

A Police Officer Recalls

ARUN PROSAD MUKHERJEE

Years ago, I was asked by a friend of mine whether I would like my two sons to join the Indian Police Service. My answer was somewhat like this : I would indeed be happy if they do so but this would have to be their own decision, and not mine. The second part of my response was that I would surely like to be 'reborn' as a member of the IPS so that I could make amends for many of the mistakes, blunders and injustices which I might have committed as also to replicate with greater determination at least some of the 'good' things which I tried to do as a police officer. This episode of nearly 20 years ago comes back to me today, perhaps with a new meaning and a new urgency.

One may justifiably ask : what is new about it or the urgency. Every police officer worth his salt must have committed mistakes and blunders and in the process might have caused injustice to some. The life of no policeman can ever be a bed of roses; the uneven path that he has to tread will more often than not be a bed of thorns. He may get an occasional bouquet if he is lucky but he can be assured of the unending stream of brickbats almost till the end of his service career. So, pray, why on earth (or heaven !) would one like to be a policeman (even as an IPS officer) again in his next birth – after having gone through the mill in this life? Some answers, though not the answer, may hopefully emerge as I go alongwith my narration.

Like most others in police profession, my service span of nearly 36 years was witness to a series of ups and downs, mercifully interspersed with valleys and plateaus, howsoever small. I got the first test of a policeman's ordeal in my very first assignment as the Sub-Divisional Police Officer (SDPO) of a politically conscious and volatile area known as the Contai subdivision of Midnapur, the biggest district then not only of West Bengal but also in India. The Left parties, at the height of their militancy, had launched the Food Movement in 1959 against the high prices and scarcity of foodgrains. The State Government, with P.C. Sen as the Congress Chief Minister, had issued instructions to the district authorities to deal with the movement 'firmly'. Well, with my lack of 'field experience' and acknowledged ignorance about jugglery of words, I interpreted 'firmly' to mean 'effectively' and preferably without use of force to the extent possible, especially, because our intelligence at the sub-division level indicated that most of the people, who would be mobilised for the demonstration by the Left parties, were a truly impoverished lot. Fortunately for me, the Sub-Divisional Officer (SDO) was a fine gentleman, of the same vintage (or rawness !) as mine, both of us having joined the IAS and the IPS, respectively, in the same year – 1956.

We two, alongwith the experienced Deputy Magistrate, the two Circle Inspectors of Police and the veteran officer-incharge of Contai Police Station discussed during the previous two days all aspects of the forthcoming episode : the approximate number of demonstrators, whether they would be carrying lathis or any other weapon of offence, who would be the leading persons for the demonstration and how they proposed to organise it and for how long. It appeared that the local leaders and organisers would like to demonstrate their ability to present a massive show of strength. It also transpired during discussions that the organisers may not like to go for a confrontation with the police and the local administration in their maiden venture of this magnitude unless they were seriously 'provoked' by the police. And that was good news for me.

Then we took stock of our available resources. The Superintendent of Police (SP), stretched as his resources were, between six sub-divisions, could spare only one platoon of the District Armed Police (i.e., one armed Sub-Inspector, one JCO, one NCO and about 25 constables); this included a Gas party of one Lance Naik and two Constables. Hence, we had to mobilise some officers and men from our other police stations, but overall the strength of our police force for dealing with a large body of persons was bound to be too inadequate and there was no prospect of additional help, for which we had tried earlier.

At this stage, and in our meeting in the evening prior to the 'big show' of the following morning, I put forward the basic outlines of our strategy and plan of action :

- Nothing should be done from our side which could provoke the demonstrators or their organisers; on the contrary, we should think of ways in which the tension among the demonstrators, at various crucial stages, could be brought down by our conscious efforts and at various points/segments of the demonstrators.
- The demonstrators would encircle the SDO's office and stage an indefinite sit-in (*gherao*) till their demands were met. The SDO's office was located at a high ground and as such its encirclement could be effectively organised by the demonstrators and thereby prevent entry and exit from the office. Hence, the SDO with his usual complement of officers and other staff members should be in the office complex from early dawn. The SDPO will also be there with a small police party. Adequate provision for food and drinking water for all of them was to be stored inside the office complex. The Probationary Assistant Magistrate (an IAS officer under training and a good singer of Bengali songs, though a South Indian) was also asked to be inside to assist the SDO and the SDPO as may be necessary. Incidentally, this turned out to be a very wise decision as subsequent events would reveal.
- The two Circle Inspectors and the OC of Contai PS

were assigned the task of controlling the three different segments of the demonstrators as was explained to them by the SDPO with the help of a hand-drawn sketch of the area of demonstration. The SDPO assured them that in spite of the *gherao*, he will be able to come out of the office complex and be in touch with the sector officers outside.

From about 7.30 the next morning, the demonstrators started converging and by about 9 a.m an unexpectedly large body of persons – men, women and children, began their sit-in demonstration with an unceasing chanting of the usual slogans castigating the government, its food policy and demanding fixation of the prices of essential commodities, especially, of paddy and rice so that these were within the purchasing power of the poor. Every half an hour or so, the SDPO could assess the crowd strength and its 'mood' from various corners of the SDO's office compound. It being on a high ground, the visibility was good and one could assess the fluctuating moods of the demonstrators at different points. Surprisingly, when the SDPO (in usual working uniform) attempted to come out of the office complex to meet some of the organisers and his officers, he was not obstructed and this, the SDPO noted, was a good sign.

The crowd all around was nearly six deep and at places even the organisers themselves found it difficult to keep them under their command, and this, too, was duly noted by the SDPO. Luckily for him, one of the organisers turned out to be a teacher of the local college and a former class-mate of the SDPO in Calcutta University. He was not the usual rabble-rouser but a fairly reasonable person, who assured the SDPO, that they would do their best to prevent any violence from their side. The SDPO, too, gave him a similar assurance so far as the police was concerned and requested this gentleman to promptly bring to his notice if any of them found anything to the contrary so that suitable remedial steps could be taken to prevent escalation of the tension.

Nevertheless, a certain level of tension was inescapable in a situation like this where several thousand people from distant villages had congregated for giving vent to their genuine grievances about non-availability or high prices of foodgrains; they were also obviously assured by their political mobilisers about the prospect of a successful conclusion through such militant mass struggle. But no such 'success' was in sight before these simple villagers even after sitting out for nearly 4-5 hours, without food or drinking water ! One could observe that their patience was running out by about 1 p.m when sections of these demonstrators started shouting at their leaders for 'not doing much to fulfil their legitimate demands'.

In course of his usual rounds of interaction with agitators, the SDPO felt that the first decisive moment had come for him to intervene lest the frustration and impatience of the hungry crowd turned into spontaneous angry outbursts or be exploited by some of the wily organisers. Any miscalculation on his part could have serious impact on both sides but some risk had to be taken to defuse the mounting tension. While observing the utterances and behaviour patterns of sections of the crowd, he thought of an 'unusual plan of action'. For implementing this, he would need the fullest cooperation of the SDO (about which the SDPO had no doubt) and also of the IAS Probationer who, too, could be coaxed into 'active participation'.

For ensuring this, he went back to SDO's office room where he found all the required 'dramatis personae' : the SDO, his senior Deputy Magistrate and the IAS Probationer, besides the SDO's PA and Bench Clerk. Incidentally, during those days before the separation of the executive and the judiciary since 1973, the SDO was also the Sub-Divisional Magistrate holding regular court for trying certain types of cases. For this purpose, a separate court room (*ejlas*) with the usual red-cloth bedecked witness box was in existence adjacent to his office room. I suggested that after some time the SDO may move to his court room with his Bench Clerk and other staff where I proposed to enact a 'drama' in the following manner : a select group of agitators alongwith one or two of the organisers would be escorted by me into the *ejlas* where they will be served some biscuits and drinking water as soon as they entered the room. Then they will be asked by the SDO to present their grievances and suggestions, which will be noted down by the SDO/SDM or by the Senior Deputy Magistrate and also by the IAS Probationer Assistant Magistrate. After having done this with due solemnity, the SDO will assure them that their grievances and suggestions will be communicated by him to the higher authorities concerned for appropriate action. After allowing them to let out their steam through the above process, the SDPO will formally thank the SDO and his officers for giving a patient hearing to the representatives of the agitators; he will also thank the demonstrators' representatives, who had taken the trouble of coming from distant villages and also for accepting his suggestion to come to the SDM's *ejlas* for ventilating their grievances instead of unnecessarily spending the whole day sitting out in the sun and that, too, without food and drink, for long hours.

If all goes well upto this stage, the SDM will declare adjournment of the court. Then the second part of the drama will be sought to be enacted with the SDPO introducing the Probationer Assistant Magistrate as a south Indian gentleman with an unusual flair for Bengali songs. Knowing the Bengali weakness for Tagore songs, he will inform the deputationists that if they so desired, the south Indian officer can be requested to sing a few Tagore songs before they go out of the court room, a very unusual but tempting proposition which few Bengalees can spurn. All these were endorsed gladly by the SDO and others.

After having made these back-stage arrangements, the SDPO walked up to that segment of the demonstrators where he had earlier observed a group of truly rustic but vocal agitators, whom even some organisers were unable to pacify. He empathised with their lot in not having anything to eat or drink for such long hours and said that he would have been happy if the organisers had made some arrangements for such elementary needs of people, who had walked long distances to come here for presenting their grievances to the appropriate authorities. This had the immediate and desired impact : the vocal section of the protestors started grilling some of the nearby organisers for their failure to provide such basic requirements and also for not appreciating some of their genuine demands. The SDPO intervened at this stage and offered them a possible solution : just by sitting here indefinitely, no useful purpose was likely to be served. Instead, if they could select from among themselves a group of about 5 to 7 persons as their representatives, they could be taken by the SDPO to the SDO-cum-SDM to whom they could put forward their genuine grievances and demand that the SDO/ SDM should bring these to the notice of the government and the higher authorities for immediate remedial steps. This was considered by them as a possible way out of the impasse and they started the process of selecting their 'genuine' representatives, much to the discomfiture of the organisers. Five such representatives were selected by the 'dissidents', disregarding the suggestion of the organisers that such selection should be left to them. In order to assuage the hurt feelings of the latter, the SDPO agreed to allow another about 3-5 persons including one of the organisers to be part of the delegation. Accompanied by one of the organisers, the SDPO could pick up at random another five persons from different segments of the assemblage, taking care to avoid such elements, who could be the usual run of militant and professional agitators.

Thus, having picked up a fairly disparate group of about eleven demonstrators plus one of the organisers who did not appear to be too troublesome, the SDPO escorted them to the august presence of the SDO-cum-SDM in the latter's *ejlas*. Then followed the carefully scripted scenario of offering them drinking water and some biscuits, and one could see the pleasant surprise writ large on the faces of the exhausted villagers. The SDPO then requested the SDM that these representatives of the aggrieved people demonstrating outside since early morning should be allowed to put forward their genuine grievances. The SDM then called upon them to convey their legitimate grievances through two or three of them who had come to meet him. The organiser began his presentation with his practised skill and oratory – how the anti-people food policy of the present government had led to further impoverishment and ruination of the poor peasantry and the other common people, how the defective and arbitrary system of levy of foodgrains (especially of paddy) had encouraged the big landholders to hoard paddy which led to further artificial push-up of paddy and rice prices and so on. He finally mentioned what, according to him, should be the fixed price of rice so that the same was within the reach of the poor villagers. At this stage, one of the 'vocal dissidents' stood up to intervene and said that the organiser was not at all correct and that the price of rice should be much less and he quoted some price, demanding that his version should be noted as the correct one. The long face of their leader was quite apparent and understandable. There were further projections of their viewpoints by another about 4-5 persons, almost each contradicting the other, especially in regard to the crucial issue of sale price of paddy and rice to be fixed by the government. The long face of the organiser displayed his embarrassment and frustration. The SDM/SDO then made his position clear by stating that the viewpoints of the representatives had been carefully noted by him and his officers and these would be sent to the higher authorities so that justice was done to them. He then adjourned the session of his court and offered some more biscuits and drinking water for the representatives.

During this recess, the SDPO introduced the senior Deputy Magistrate and the IAS Probationer Assistant Magistrate, emphasising the south Indian origin of the latter and his excellent mastery over Bengali songs in general, and Tagore songs in particular. If they so desired, the SDPO stated, this gentleman could be persuaded to sing a couple of Tagore songs for them in this very room. Their faces brightened up and the SDO made the predetermined request to his junior colleague to offer one or two Tagore songs. And then followed for the next 15 minutes the unprecedented spectacle of a music session in the SDM's *ejlas*, much to the delight of the erstwhile agitators. There was a distinct change in their mood when they were taken out by the SDPO and presented before the rest of the sit-in demonstrators. The SDPO explained the proceedings in the SDM's *ejlas*, namely, projection of their grievances by members of the delegation, the assurance by the SDO that their viewpoints would be duly communicated very early to the higher authorities for necessary action since the SDO was not competent to fix the prices of paddy and rice as desired by them and, finally, the brief music session which feted their representatives. There was a distinct look of disbelief and amusement among the assemblage but most of them burst out laughing when some of their representatives confirmed what the SDPO had narrated.

At this stage the SDPO addressed the available organisers to say that since their demands had been met so far as it was feasible at the sub-division level and they had also registered their grievances, it would be in the fitness of things if the assembled people could be asked now to disperse and go back to their villages. Despite some expected humming and hawing by a few organisers, the demonstrators who were already tired of their exertions without any food and drink, started moving out of the area. But one of the organisers had some other motivation – to display some show of militancy by having a show-down with the police and the administration. Thus, he alongwith about five hundred of his followers refused to go away and continued with the *gherao* and the demonstration.

This led to another round of discussion between the SDO, the SDPO and other senior civil and police officers. It was nearly five in the afternoon. The SDPO explained that all his officers and men had been out on the ground almost since six in the morning, most of them being without food and without any break. As such, their patience was likely to be somewhat fragile and they may be tempted for a course of action which will shorten their ordeal. The physical and mental condition of the demonstrators, the SDPO noted, would be even worse and they, too, were likely to be edgy and likely to play into the hands of the wily organiser by picking up a fight on some pretext or the other which may result in unnecessary violence. All the officers present endorsed the assessment of the SDPO as realistic. At the request of the SDO, the SDPO spelt out their options : half of the mobilised police force on duty would be given immediate stand-down and asked to re-assemble at two specified points after an hour – after they had a bath, something to eat and also take some rest, howsoever brief; on their return, the remaining portion of the force, closed at two strategic points instead of remaining widely dispersed as in the morning till then, would be released for an hour as in the case of the first group. In other words, after about two and half hours, the entire refreshed force would be available for dealing with any emerging situation. During this intervening period, the senior police officers (alas, only four in number – the SDPO, the two Circle Inspectors and the OC of Contai PS !) alongwith a skeleton staff would have to hold the ground and not allow the remnants of the demonstrators to indulge in any precipitate outbursts.

Operationally, the SDPO further explained, they had two options provided they could prevent any violence or disorder during the two and half an hour interregnum. The first one was the traditional one : give due warnings to the agitators that they should disperse peacefully within the next fifteen minutes or so, failing which, they would be declared as an unlawful assembly as provided under law and then police would disperse them by using such force as may be necessary. The use of tear gas and lathi charge by the police could follow, resulting in removal of the agitators. But it would be night by the time such action could take place and no one could prevent at least some of the dispersing agitators from sneaking into lanes and bye-lanes and resorting to sporadic acts of violence like ransacking or looting of or setting fire to some shops. This could set in motion, the usual cycle of violence and counter-violence, the prevention of which had been uppermost in their mind.

The second option and the preferred one, according to the SDPO, was to leave this relatively small group of agitators alone, virtually 'ignoring' them publicly but keeping a sharp eye on them from some vantage points at discreet distance. Around midnight, when they were most likely to be off guard and thoroughly exhausted, it may not be difficult for a well-organised police party under the leadership of the SDPO assisted by one of the Circle Inspectors, the OC, Contai PS and the Armed SI with about fifty policemen to suddenly start chasing them with a full-throated battle-cry, enough to scare away even trained and militant agitators at such unearthly hour of the night. Another police party under the other Circle Inspector would have taken up position in advance so as to prevent the fleeing agitators from entering into the nearby lanes and bye-lanes or from indulging in any mischief after being thus dispersed. Hopefully, the use of any lethal arms by the police should not be necessary, the SDPO concluded. All the assembled officers gave their reactions, almost fully agreeing with the second and preferred option outlined by the SDPO. And, luckily for all, the day's ordeal ended well past midnight and as planned, much to every one's relief.

However, the above narration may give a wrong impression that the SDO and the SDPO had a smooth sailing throughout the day. Far from it. For, they were continuously engaged in warding off 'attacks' from other quarters. The three districts of West Bengal – Midnapur, 24-Paraganas and Burdwan, contributed the largest number of members to the Legislative Assembly and were known as the 'king-maker districts'. Two of the important 'king-makers' were residents of Contai. They had expected the local administration including the police to deal with the demonstrators 'firmly' by resorting to the traditional police methods and not allowing them to 'paralyse' the administration. When they failed at the local level to convince us about the inescapability or dire urgency of resorting to traditional strong-arm methods instead of our unconventional 'trial-of-patience' technique, they conveyed their displeasure to the seat of power in Calcutta. Soon the alarm bells started ringing at the district Headquarters in Midnapur. The District Magistrate and the SP, followed by the ADM/ Additional SP began contacting us over phone and the wireless at almost hourly intervals, wanting to know when did we propose to disperse the unruly mob. Both of us informed our respective bosses politely that the demonstrators were not yet an 'unruly mob' and we were quite confident till then to be able to disperse them in due course, preferably without recourse to force. Obviously, they could not have been pleased with our response and we were informed that another contingent of about 20-30 armed policemen under the charge of an Armed Inspector will reach us in the next two hours to assist us in the task of quick dispersal of the agitators. Not too bad, we thought and kept our fingers crossed and our powder dry to meet any unforeseen eventuality.

When the fateful day's proceedings including the musical interlude and the midnight 'bloodless coup' became public knowledge the next morning, even the two 'king-makers' of Contai, besides the local people cutting across party lines, were unstinted in their approbation of our unusual methodology in defusing a potentially explosive situation without firing even a single shot. This was considered especially remarkable when it became known that perhaps Contai was the only sensitive sub-division, where the police did not have to open fire in dealing with the agitators of the militant food movement organised by all the Left parties in West Bengal.

For nearly a year thereafter during his continuance as Contai's SDPO, the residents of most of the villages which he visited vied with each other in offering a cup of tea or a green coconut to him. It was their way of saying "thank you for sparing us a violent ending to our legitimate quest for justice". Honestly speaking, I could not have hoped for a more satisfying reward from any other quarter.

3

An Early Lesson in Leadership

A.K. DAVE

A disgruntled Sub Inspector in Amravati District of M.P. carried out a raid in the year 1950 on a gambling den which was located outside his jurisdiction in order to bring about an exposure of the alleged links of the then Superintendent of Police with the politicians behind the den. As AIG, Anti-Corruption, I was asked to initiate a confidential enquiry. It led to circumstantial support for the allegation and the orders of the transfer of the SP followed. Almost simultaneously, the IG of Police being asked to effect economies in police expenditure, offered to close down the Anti-corruption Branch which, as he told me, he was sure the government could never agree to on account of public reaction. But to his surprise, the proposal was immediately accepted. I suspect this was because the Branch had succeeded in filing a larger number of prosecutions and reports for departmental enquiries than was anticipated. What was more, it had begun to receive some information about a few high level, politically sensitive shady deals. I was thus available for posting and was sent to relieve the very SP whose conduct had come under review. My taking charge was not popular with the middle Indian National Congress leadership of the district which included, amongst others, a prominent Muslim bus and truck operator, who was an MP. Those were the days of *de facto* one party rule. Ministers and most of the MLAs and MPs were familiar with the system of administration and were unwilling to undermine them. Bureaucracy was by and large honest and committed to good governance.

Within a few days of being incharge, the MP approached me to nominate a certain SI in the city for promotion as a Circle Inspector. The SI had the necessary length of service but I had noticed a certain carelessness in investigations and had decided to watch his performance before taking up his case for promotion. But the MP was insistent and repeatedly claimed that "Dada", the very distinguished litterateur and popular, Veer Waman Rao Joshi, leader of the Congress in Berar and residing in Amravati and on whom I had called soon after taking charge, had asked him to request me to nominate the SI. I told him I was sure Dada would leave the decision to me. But he was not to be put off. To put an end to the discussion, I told the MP that the SI was in need of experience in a Tahsil Police Station before earning a nomination and that I had accordingly already ordered his transfer the previous day and given him the opportunity to prove himself in the next six months. This abruptly terminated the meeting and, in fact, I had no other approaches of the kind thereafter from any quarter. Retribution from the party in power for non-conformance was virtually non-existent those days.

About a month later, the City Inspector (there were only two City Superintendents in the Province, at Nagpur and Jabalpur) rang me up early in the morning to report that in a Muslim locality, which was close to a refugee Sindhi habitation, two cows had been slaughtered in the courtyard of a house. There was some tension in the area and he had posted staff as a preventive measure. He expected no trouble. The DIG was also informed as was the District Magistrate and the Divisional Commissioner by the City Inspector. The DIG did briefly discuss the matter with me and did not consider it necessary to give any advice.

That was the day my sister was arriving from Nagpur to help me look after my wife who was down with typhoid. She had to be received at the Badnera railway station at about 10.00 a.m. as she was travelling by herself. Badnera is six miles away from Amravati. I verified from the City Inspector at 9.00 a.m. that the situation was quiet and then drove myself to the station to get her. The train arrived a few minutes late. I searched up and down the train but she was not on board. After the train left, I got back to the car and proceeded to Amravati. Barely two miles later, I could see thick black smoke rising above the town. My immediate thought was that the city was in flames and rioting was on.

I drove to the centre of the town and stopped at a prominent T-junction, which had a road leading to the possible site of rioting. I was dressed in the usual working dress of those days which was a half-sleeve check shirt and grey trousers. Right in front of me, at the very corner of the T-junction, a mob was trying to break open a prominent Muslim's shop. I went forward, shouted at the miscreants, got hold of the hand of one who was wielding an iron rod to break down the door and took it away. The effect was electric for they ran away. Then, as I walked down the road to the site of rioting, I was joined by one constable and then a little later by another who, despite my lack of uniform, had no difficulty in identifying me. As I reached the site, I saw that a couple of houses were burning, a godown full of varnish and paints was spewing black smoke and the nearest cotton godowns were beginning to catch fire. There was a petrol bunk in between but fortunately there was no sign of fire there. I also saw that the strike force had already reached from the Reserve Lines and had been deployed. Rioting had stopped. Three men had been murdered and a couple injured. The situation was under control but the danger of the fire spreading was growing. The city municipality had a fire station equipped with bullock carts to carry water to quench any fire. May be, it could save a part of a house on fire in an emergency. Just then the Sangh Chalak of the Rashtriya Swayam Sewak Sangh of Amravati district, Dr. Agarwal, if I recall the name correctly, was going past on his motorcycle possibly to survey the area and seeing me immediately stopped and asked if his boys could be of any help. I told him that his boys might well be more of a problem because of the Muslim presence in the locality. He assured me that they would be disciplined and I need not fear any misbehaviour or provocation from them. I then quite readily agreed and requested him for his help to deal with the spreading fire. I was very afraid that godowns containing bales of cotton, the main produce of the region, might go up in flames if the fire was not suppressed. Within 15-20 minutes, about 20 Rashtriya Swayam Sewak Sangh volunteers turned up and were asked by me to get on the roof tops to isolate the godowns and prevent the fire from spreading and help put out the fire. Their response was immediate. They clambered up to the roofs of the godowns pulled down connecting tin sheets and rafters through which the fire could spread. In less than an hour, the threat of fire spreading beyond the affected paint godown was over. Meanwhile, water carts of the municipality had also arrived and helped douse the fire. Thus, ended the rioting. Investigation commenced. A few suspected culprits were rounded up.

It was only too clear to me that I had been extremely rash in leaving the city even for an hour on such a day when cows had been slaughtered and tensions could get out of hand. I was sure that an enquiry would soon follow. Anticipating further that the City Inspector and his staff might be tempted to fudge the police records and falsify the documents to ensure their defence, I called the City Inspector for a briefing.

I explained to him that I was very much at fault having left the town; and that he too was at fault for misjudging the possibility of the outbreak and in assuring me that matters were under control. But after the initial and grave errors committed, the police as a whole had performed efficiently. The strike force had arrived promptly and acted swiftly. Order was restored and the damage to property minimised. There was no looting. I said the net result of an enquiry that very likely would be ordered would be that I would be awarded a "Censure" in my confidential roll and he would suffer a major penalty such as reduction in pay by two increments apart from being transferred. I was willing to accept my punishment and I expected him to do the same. I also confidently assured him that his record was good and there was no reason why his promotion as Deputy Superintendent of Police, which was due, would get delayed by more than six months to an year following the enquiry. I got his assurance that there would be no falsification of records.

The local press, especially the pro-Congress daily and weekly, carried a campaign of criticism of the police for its failure. Prominent amongst the critics and their patrons were those who had been deprived of their share of income from the gambling den which had had to close down after the SI's raid. It was too good an opportunity for them to miss to get their own back.

The enquiry was initiated a little later when the Muslims approached Maulana Abul Kalam Azad, then a Minister in the Central Cabinet, who took up their case with the Prime Minister. The State Government had no choice but to order an enquiry. Having made sure that there would be no falsification of documents and being ready to accept responsibility, I was not unduly concerned.

A couple of days before the enquiry was to open, 'Dada' Veer Waman Rao Joshi himself accompanied by the District Congress Secretary came to my house and in a fatherly way said, "Anand, why did you not tell me that your wife has been so ill. You tell us what you want us to do and say at the enquiry". The Secretary of the District Congress too assured me of full help in whatever way I needed. I thanked them for their kindness in offering to help but said that I did not think I needed any. Nevertheless, Dada pressed me to take their help to put up witnesses who would say whatever I would like them to say to defend the police. I again declined the offer and thanked him for his consideration. Two days later, the enquiry commenced.

Shri K.P. Mushran, IAS, a Member of the Revenue Board, was the Inquiry Officer. He examined the City Inspector and some other junior members of the police force to begin with, I was gratified to note that they did not try to put forward any artful defence but stuck to the facts as they had occurred. Thereafter, I gave my evidence.

Witnesses from the public were those who had witnessed the occurrence of riots and those who had expressed themselves in critical and condemnatory articles and editorials of the local newspapers. He was good enough to allow me to put questions to them in order to get the facts straight. Some of them were members of, or closely associated with, the Congress Party. They toned down the criticism of the police. Some even blamed the Muslims for provocative conduct and goondaism.

There were Muslim witnesses, too, including a few, who were believed to have been involved in the slaughter of cows, and notably those, who had directly suffered from the rioting, including the owners of the paint and varnish store and the relations of those who had lost their lives. One or two cotton godown owners, who had suffered some losses, also gave evidence. In answer to my questions, they hotly denied any links with Pakistan and of any plans to migrate with their families. At this stage, letters intercepted well before the rioting from the prominent Muslim witnesses to their relations in Pakistan, conveying their decision to migrate shortly, were presented by me to the Inquiry Officer. Their evidence became suspect and reduced the impact of their critical comments about the police handling of the outbreak of the riots.

I must say that neither I nor the non-gazetted staff allowed the enquiry to affect our routine work in anyway. Our conscience was clear that we had not given any false evidence nor had induced anyone else to do so. The rest of the force also retained its morale.

Mr. B.L. Pyasi, the City Inspector, was transferred a month after the conclusion of the enquiry to an equivalent post. After examining the report of the Inquiry Officer and taking into account the comments on it given by the Inspector General of Police, the Government awarded only a "Censure" as punishment to him. He was promoted as a Deputy Superintendent of Police soon after. I somehow escaped punishment. No adverse entry in my character roll was made and communicated to me. I might add that I did not excuse myself for my failure to act wisely and with due caution. The entire episode, in the ultimate analysis, did not affect my progression in my career in subsequent years. This itself was very heartening. It reinforced my belief that honesty, integrity, transparency, political neutrality and moral courage to accept guilt when necessary was a sound principle of leadership.

Value of Negative Example

We have all heard of Heroes of Labour and other heroes that were glamourised by the Communist Parties, specially those of the Soviet Union and China. However, it is to the Communist Party of China that one has to give the credit for coining the expression "learning by negative example". The party would highlight the failures of a particular person and by publicising them call upon the rank and file to understand the nature of the mistakes made and learn how such mistakes were to be avoided. Since its conflict began with the Communist Party of Soviet Union, the Communist Party of China itself learned a lot from the latter by its several "negative examples" in ideology and action. I recall an incident very early in my career as a Superintendent of Police, which became for me personally and for all those I subsequently had a chance to advise, as one of the most useful and practical "negative examples".

Babu Rajendra Prasad, the then President of the Indian National Congress, was to come to Jabalpur at the invitation of the State Congress Party in order to lay the foundation stone of the Martyrs' Memorial in the large Gol Bazaar ground at Jabalpur in the year 1948. I was then the Senior Superintendent of Police. The luminaries who had organised the event were Seth Govind Das, MP and Shri Laxmi Shankar Bhatt at Jabalpur. The Chief Minister, Shri Ravi Shankar Shukla and the Home Minister, Shri D.P. Mishra were to come from Nagpur, the then state capital.

The District Magistrate, Shri R.R. Bahl, ICS, and I were told by Seth Govind Das that the Congress Party would be managing the entire event on its own utilising the services of a large body of Congress Swayam Sewaks. They did not want any police assistance or any "government" arrangements whatsoever to be made. This would be below the dignity of the local Congress unit. They were so confident that we accepted their claim after a preliminary site survey and a quick scrutiny of the details of the programme.

The ceremony was to begin with the laying of the foundation stone by Babu Rajendra Prasad. Thereafter, he was to address a meeting within the same ground about 75 yards away. The public was to be confined to the meeting area.

Babu Rajendra Prasad was delayed and arrived an hour late. He was not in good health. The convenors decided to reverse the sequence and took him straight to the elevated platform. There he sat resting against bolsters and was given an injection to control his asthmatic attack. The Chief Minister and others on the dais kept looking at him, rather concerned about his fitness for the ordeal of addressing the masses. Seth Govind Dass initiating the proceedings addressed the gathering of some 70-100 thousand persons. People were in a happy mood and relaxed. The British had left and there were no enemies to denounce. It appeared as if the entire city had turned up. The enthusiasm of the masses on having achieved Independence was so great. They wanted to be a party to the erection of the Martyrs' Memorial. The people sat on the ground quite close to the platform. I can visual the scene of the dais. Pt. Ravi Shankar Shukla, tall, fair and handsome in pure white, with an impressive white moustache and a benign presence that immediately inspired respect without intimidation. He was amongst the very few political personalities of those days to sport an *Angavastram*. He draped it elegantly once round the neck and then let it flow down in front on one side up to the knees; Pt. D.P. Mishra, slim and simple, his super intellect well-concealed, dressed in a long cream coat, which in those days was popular with the gentry for social functions. What a command over Hindi in his speech and a refined, subtle sense of humour so very pleasing to the ear.

When sufficiently recovered from the asthmatic attack, Babu Rajendra Prasad remained seated and addressed the public meeting for about 20 minutes. A mild self-effacing personality, tall and dignified, he had outstanding academic record and profound understanding of Indian affairs hidden behind the visage of rural India. The utter simplicity of the man called out for spontaneous homage. His speech, also in simple Hindi, was inspiring, persuading the masses to rise above themselves.

Thereafter, the dignitaries came down the steps and slowly proceeded towards the small enclosure of just 50′ × 50′ made up of iron pipes, within which the foundation stone was to be laid. Freed from the necessity to remain seated at the public meeting, the massive audience soon began to move along and ahead of the dignitaries. The Swayam Sewaks made every effort to keep them insulated from the pressure of the crowd. They managed to get them to the enclosure and the ceremony of laying the foundation stone began.

By this time, we had collected about 15 policemen inside the enclosure and were trying hard to keep people away from entering and jumping over the low fence and disrupting the ceremony. Persons within were jostling to get close to the centre of the ceremony and out-shouting each other in sheer exuberance and excitement. I remember pushing a person so hard in order to keep him out of the enclosure that he screamed and I suddenly realised with a sense of shock that he was already inside and his back was against the railing and I was about to snap his spine ! There was confusion all around and no possibility of restoring order.

As the sacred Sanskrit chants accompanied the installation of the foundation stone, the crowds increased. The brick platform was completed. Then, the stone plaque placed in position and duly a trowel or two of cement mortar pressed around one corner by Babu Rajendra Prasad. Meanwhile, I began the exercise of organising the few policemen available to escort the dignitaries out through the milling crowd. Perhaps, a couple of Sub-Inspectors and a dozen constables were all that I could find. We formed an inner cordon with constables holding their lathis together as a moving railing. Just outside was a parallel cordon of the Congress Swayam Sewaks also trying to do the same. It is horrifying to recall how as we moved out of the enclosure, the crowd surged forward for the 'darshan' of the venerated political leaders. I was sure that at some stage the cordon would break and we would fail to protect them from being mobbed and who knows even trampled upon. Pt. Shukla in front, Babu Rajendra Prasad right behind with Shri Bhatt, a strong young Congress leader by his side and then Shri D.P. Mishra, all in slow motion. Babu Rajendra Prasad was weaker than when he had arrived and the distance to be covered was quite long. The dust in the air was enough to aggravate his condition. There was no question of making a fast get away. Nor was there any chance of getting their vehicles into the grounds through the crowd. Slowly and steadily, we made our way and finally managed to reach the cars and get them away to safety.

The Deputy Commissioner and I both realised what a great mistake we had made in leaving the planning and the arrangements to the local Congress leadership and accepting an assurance that they were quite capable of managing the event properly and agreeing not to interfere or even participate in the planning. Never again would we take any such assurances for granted. In fact, we should have realised that in every public gathering, it was clearly the duty of the district administration, especially the police, to participate in the details of planning of any public event and to be firm in refusing to get persuaded against their better judgment to permit the organisers to assume that they by themselves could adequately and assuredly handle an event and any hazards to safety that might arise.

Today, perhaps, this lesson hardly needs to be stated for every congregation of people requires careful police preparation for prevention of disorder and injury to life and limb. Anticipating foreseen and unforeseen ramifications of any policy and planning decision or event likely to affect security and public order has become very much an acquired skill for the All India Services as a whole.

4

The Case of an Old Woman

S.V.M. TRIPATHI

My actual promotion in the senior scale of Indian Police Service was delayed by about three months. According to the practice then prevailing, I was earmarked and posed as Deputy Central Intelligence Officer, Intelligence Bureau at Delhi in early 1965 in view of my rank in the all-India list of 1961 batch of IPS. At that time I was working at Lucknow as Deputy Assistant to Inspector General of Police, UP. It so happened that two of my distinguished immediate predecessors, occupying similar high all-India rankings in their batches, had also been earmarked and had taken up their assignments in the Intelligence Bureau. Shri Shanti Prasad, IG, UP, felt that young police officers should start working in the Intelligence Bureau only after they have acquired some experience as District Superintendent of Police. As I had not enough personal experience of district policing and none of IB, I felt a little flattered, as it appeared that he valued my usefulness enough to write to the concerned authorities that I should be allowed to remain in the state. When I got a little flustered at the earlier promotion of my batch mate, immediately below me in the civil list, as Additional Superintendent of Police, Lucknow, Shri Shanti Prasad told me not to bother as I would retain my original seniority and my pay would, in any case, be protected under the "next below" Rule. He also mentioned, nearly two months prior to the event, that I would be posted to an independent charge as Superintendent of Police, Mathura, as soon as this matter of earmarking was sorted out to his satisfaction.

I joined as Superintendent of Police, Mathura on October 17, 1965, with a total service of less than 4½ years, and at a young age of a little over 27 years. The sage words of Shri Shanti Prasad – "Show your face to the public as frequently as possible at all times of the day and night, meet freely the maximum number of persons, including policemen, formally and informally, and try to help them" – were still ringing in my ears. Amongst the very large number of persons who met me in the first week at Mathura was a middle-aged widow belonging to a landed family of Rajputs residing at Naujhil. For the purpose of this narration, we will call her Smt. Savitri Devi. Apparently, she was not able to fix on a proper pigeon-hole where she could place me initially. She addressed me sometimes as 'son', sometimes as 'Kaptan Saheb' and even occasionally as 'Pandit Ji'! The last epithet added to my obvious embarrassment.

She had a tale of woe common to women almost all over the world but which is 'redoubled in spades' for women without an adult male family member in Indian rural areas. She owned substantial agricultural land and was working her fields through sub-contracts. The three or four families of her husband's cousins, being numerically strong and wielding considerable muscle power, were creating various hurdles, presumably with a view to driving her out of the village so that they could usurp her property. Smt. Savitri Devi had only two young daughters about whose safety she was particularly worried. Her opponents had encroached upon some of her plots of land, had interfered with her right of way by creating obstructions on a street and were generally abusive in their behaviour. Like all government servants, who are unsure of their immediate course of action, I decided to advise her about the rules. In this manner, I was also following my natural inclination of not involving police in matters of civil nature. I told her that she could lodge reports of the criminal acts, which appeared to be non-cognisable, at the Police Station and canvass her civil and revenue problems in the appropriate courts. The lady was sceptical but promised to follow my advice. She told me that she reserved her right to come back to me if it did not work.

In the whirl of activities relating to familiarisation with the problems of a new district, the police force and the people of the area I lost track of this matter for some time. Mathura was full of historical places and innumerable temples and visit to these places replete with history was both a duty and pleasure. A very large number of religious festivals required massive police arrangements. It was an old garrison town and in the aftermath of 1965 war with Pakistan the presence of the army in Mathura was in the process of quantum upgradation. This required substantive modification in liaison and security apparatus in the Cantonment area. Smt. Savitri Devi reappeared before me after another ten days. In a tone, which was only partly wheedling but full of sorrow, she mentioned that her opponents had also started taunting her about the ineffectiveness of approaching the authorities. As expected no action had been taken on her reports at the Police Station and she was able to lodge a case before the Sub-Divisional Magistrate after considerable difficulty and at great expense. Her lawyer had informed her that it is too soon to expect any result in these court cases. "Kaptan Saheb", she said in despair, "if you cannot help me, nobody can". As I was in a hurry to leave for Agra to attend a meeting called by the DIG of Police I promised to see what could be done in her case by the police. Against my natural instinct, her pathetic pleas convinced me that informal proactive action is required to help this old lady. I decided to give the task of persuading her opposite parties to behave themselves to the Station House Officer of Naujhil police station. Of the sixteen police stations in Mathura in 1965, Naujhil was the only one, which I had not visited till then, probably as it was the farthest from the district headquarters. On return from Agra, I planned to visit the police station at the earliest. I indicated my tentative programme of visit to Smt. Savitri Devi also so that, in case she felt the need, she could see me there.

I paid the overdue visit to Naujhil within the next two days and gave instructions to the SHO about this matter. He obliquely mentioned that the opponents of Smt. Savitri Devi were not bad people but he will sort out the matter and report to me. After making a casual inspection of the police station and talking individually to each policeman posted there, I also held a meeting of respectable citizens of the area and enquired about any local problems, which they may be facing. Names of a few persons, who habitually threw their weight about, and were in a way feared by the local populace, came up during this meeting. I looked up the concerned police station records but did not find any mention of these names. The SHO also did not give any indication that these persons were, in any way, connected with the parties allegedly harassing the old lady. After about a week, the SHO reported to me that he had spoken to the parties concerned, including Smt. Savitri Devi, and that the matter had been sorted out. All concerned agreed that there would be no harassment to the lady and her family. The civil matters pending before the courts would, of course, take their own time.

Immediately afterwards the lady paid another visit to my residence and reiterated that the harassment continued unabated. The parties had agreed to whatever had been proposed by the SHO and had behaved better for a couple of days. However, they had gone back on their words. On my specific query she gave the names of all the family members and supporters of her opposite parties. As some of the names appeared vaguely familiar to me I looked into the record of the meeting with the citizens at Naujhil and found that two of these were the same as those given out at the meeting as persons who generally indulged in high-handed behaviour. I then called the SHO and the Deputy Superintendent of Police, incharge of the circle, and instructed them to warn the opposite parties again and ensure that they did not go back to their old ways. The police officers even suggested that the problem might be more effectively tackled if the aggressors were involved in substantive criminal cases. It was left unsaid but presumably these would be false cases. Only for one moment was I tempted to acquiesce in this unlawful short cut. Almost in mid-stride I remembered the homilies I had been dishing out to police officers in my district never to resort to such short cuts. This was a course of action, therefore, which I expressly forbade but said, with as stern a countenance as I could muster, that they would be responsible for the safety of the old lady and her family. Their warnings had only a fleeting effect as was mentioned by the old lady on her third visit to Mathura. After a lull of about a fortnight her opponents had again started their abusive and obnoxious behaviour.

Going a little out of the way, I thereafter called the concerned Sub-Divisional Magistrate, a Deputy Collector, who had come on his first regular posting to Mathura. I gave him the details of the case and asked him to look into the matters pending in his court at an early date and to direct his tahsil staff to verify the allegations of encroachments and obstructions. If he found that the problems allegedly faced by the old woman were correct, he should restore the *status quo* on the ground and warn the offending parties. The SDM, being even younger than me, enthusiastically promised to see that the complaints of the old woman would be fully and finally attended to. I even made a casual mention of this problem to the District Magistrate (actually more than twice my age !), who gently mentioned that such problems generally disappeared with time and that I had done all that was possible. The SDM met me after a while and said that he had not yet received the report of the tahsil staff and would definitely take action as soon as it was forthcoming. He also obliquely mentioned about the political backing, which the parties opposed to Smt. Savitri Devi had with them. I could sense that his resolve to do the right thing was in jeopardy.

All this drama had consumed over two months. Late December can be bitterly cold in Mathura. On Sunday, December 26, 1965, in the aftermath of a rollicking Christmas party held in an Army Mess, I went out very early after a skimpy "Chota Haazri", to visit one scene each of a murder and a dacoity. I was under the impression that it would be possible to return home for lunch as reportedly both cases had been "worked out" already. It was largely a matter of satisfying oneself whether the investigations are proceeding on right lines. Things got somewhat sticky in the case of dacoity, where I found that at least one arrested person had been wrongly implicated by the complainant. After talking to all the witnesses and reviewing the case fully with the investigating officer, the supervising officer and the public prosecutor, it was decided to send a report for the release of this particular person under Section 169 CrPC to the court.

I reached back at 1700 hrs., almost without food for the whole day. It was already getting dark. The first sight, which met my eyes, as I was about to alight from the Jeep, was that of Smt. Savitri Devi, shivering in cold and bitterly weeping. She came rushing to me and caught both my feet imploring that she and her family members should be killed, as she had no right to live! When she calmed down to some extent she informed that she had been waiting for me since almost mid-day. In the morning 4-5 persons belonging to the opposite party had come to her place abused and beat her and even her two daughters. She showed the resultant bruises. They kept harping on the theme that if she kept complaining to authorities worse fate would befall her family. She would be better off if she just went away. They even mentioned a sum of about three thousand rupees, which they were willing to give to her if she complied with their demands. They threatened dire consequences if she did not take their offer. She had kept her daughters with the family of her neighbours and had come directly to Mathura.

To say that I over-reacted would be an understatement. I did not even go inside my residence and just picked up the uniform greatcoat from the verandah as a protection against chilly winds encountered in a Jeep journey. Apart from my driver I had only a head constable with a Thompson carbine. I invited Smt. Savitri Devi to sit in the Jeep and come with me. I left immediately for Naujhil, picking up additional fuel on the way. I asked to be taken directly to the house of the main member of the opposite party. At Naujhil, where we reached around 1900 hrs, I spotted a police chowkidar who was returning after his fortnightly attendance at the police station. I directed him to fetch the SHO, alongwith as many men as he could muster at the police station, and bring them to the house to which I was proceeding directly. When I arrived at my destination, I found a palatial double-storied house. I shouted that the head of this household should come out at once, which he immediately did and invited me inside. Refusing the invitation rudely, I asked him to fetch the other leaders of the families involved in the complaint. Having got these persons assembled within 10 minutes, I let go and roundly cursed them for harassing the old lady. I told them that this must stop otherwise I shall visit their place in two day's time and personally give physical chastisement. For good measure I told them that they have to visit the court of the Sub-Divisional Magistrate tomorrow and give an undertaking that they concede the claim made by Smt. Savitri Devi, get this undertaking ratified by the court and inform me personally at Mathura that this has been done. If I received even a false complaint that they have misbehaved with any member of her family they will have to answer to me. All the time I behaved in a threatening and even reckless manner, which was totally against my natural character. In the meanwhile the SHO had also arrived with about half a dozen policemen. I made him responsible for ensuring that all this was complied with and that the old lady and her family were installed safely in her house.

Having done with my piece I left Naujhil at 2100 hrs. and finally arrived at my residence two hours later. On the way back, when I cooled down a little, I pondered over the consequences of my actions. I decided that if the people aggrieved with my behaviour filed a complaint in any court I should accept whatever had actually transpired, including the threats that I had held out and the abusive behaviour. I would, however, clarify the provocation for this action and try to show my bonafide intention, which was to help a person who really needed such help. I had decided to speak the truth steadfastly. Even then I was a troubled man as many, who habitually derided the practice of sending practically raw officers as Superintendents of Police, could use this incident. Most importantly, I felt that if this incident got out of my hands I would have belied the trust of IG, UP.

In those days in UP, rural police stations did not have radio contact with district headquarters and also did not have telephones. The constable, who brought the daily papers from the police station, carried word from the SHO that all leaders of the opposite party were preparing to go to the court of the Sub-Divisional Magistrate. Smt. Savitri Devi was also going with them. I spoke to the SDM to see that adequate time was given to complete the required formalities. In the evening, about 10 persons, mostly belonging to the party inimical to Smt. Savitri Devi, alongwith her came to my residence. They had complied with all that I had demanded and the SDM had ratified the formal agreement. They also promised that in future no complaint would reach me on this account. I was a very happy but also a relieved man. The office of District Superintendent of Police carried enough prestige to dissuade any person from going to the court over the misbehaviour of a young man. For good measure they also invited me to a traditional meal of "Dal and Bati", which I formally accepted. Smt. Savitri Devi told me, "Son, I knew that if you could not help me, no one could".

There must be a moral to this story ! Only I do not want to spell it out and spoil the career of any young police officer, who may be tempted to adopt a similar course of action. If he follows his heart and instincts, as I did, he is more than likely to come to grief. Many things have changed since 1965. Overeager and sometimes aggressive media, particularly the electronic media, has to 'discover' some motive, largely on the baser side, if any government functionary takes any unusual step. It will find any number of "experts" eulogizing or decrying agonising decisions, taken by officers on the spot. Official prestige, which bestowed some immunity against political power, is no longer sufficient to give protection. Money and muscle power, which the party opposing Smt. Savitri Devi had in significant measure, cannot always be nullified solely by official response these days.

However, in hindsight, the actions taken in this episode, still give me warm and wonderful feeling of satisfaction !

5

Through Heat and Dust in UP

PRAKASH SINGH

While holding the charge of Director General of Police, Uttar Pradesh, I was once asked by a journalist to identify the three major problems I was confronting. I thought for a second and then replied: (1) communalism, (2) terrorism, and (3) a section of senior IPS officers. The journalist was flabbergasted at the mention of the third component and wanted me to elucidate. I told him that these officers were waiting for my ouster or departure and were indulging in all kinds of dirty tricks to facilitate that process so that one of them could occupy the coveted seat of Director General. It may appear a harsh indictment of senior officers, but for me it was an unfortunate reality. While battling with the multifarious problems which the state threw up, I had at the same time to contend with the enemy within. It is a sad reflection on the team spirit of IPS officers. What Shakespeare called "overvaulting ambition" gets the better of their sense of camaraderie.

However, let me first write at some length on the other two problems which took my maximum time and attention.

Communalism

The Bharatiya Janata Party (BJP) had been voted to power in UP in mid-1991 and Kalyan Singh was the Chief Minister. The communal atmosphere in the state was quite delicate. Soon after I had taken charge, the Chief Minister called a meeting of all the Secretaries, Commissioners and senior police officers including DIGs incharge Ranges. We were asked to speak and identify the major problems in our respective jurisdictions. I remember Commissioner after Commissioner rising and talking of every problem under the sun except the communal problem. Apparently, they were scared of saying anything which might offend the ruling party. When my turn came, I mentioned communal situation as the problem number one for the police. I still recall senior bureaucrats raising their eyebrows at my presentation. However, I was not daunted and continued with my dissertation. At the end of the conference, while we were dispersing for lunch, about 7 or 8 young IAS officers congratulated me for my bold expression of views – something which they had found missing among their own top brass.

The Ram Janma Bhoomi/Babri Masjid controversy was the most complex part of the communal imbroglio. The Bharatiya Janata Party, the Vishwa Hindu Parishad and the Bajrang Dal were committed to building Ram Temple at the disputed place. A security scheme for the Ram Janma Bhoomi/Babri Masjid (RJB/BM) complex had been prepared by the Intelligence Bureau and submitted to the Government of UP in early 1991. Its recommendations were by and large implemented.

The administration was under tremendous pressure to relax the security arrangements at the disputed shrine. One of the ministers, who is tragically no more, (Brahma Dutt Dwivedi) was particularly aggressive in mounting pressure on the state police. At a high level meeting held on December 28, 1991, we were almost ordered that the portable barrier/ rope which had been placed to regulate crowd at the space below the three domes should be removed, that the obstruction between Singh Dwar and Kaushalya Rasoi should be done away with, etc. We, however, firmly resisted some other suggestions like removal of concertina coils on the stairs going up the domes, that frisking of persons should be selective, and some others. I found it very galling that the senior bureaucrats, particularly the Chief Secretary, took a very soft line at these discussions and were conveniently amenable to the wishes and recommendations of the political leadership. I was the odd man out, protesting against the suggestions which I thought would jeopardise the security of the structure. The political leadership started feeling – though they never said so openly – that I would not fall in line in the implementation of whatever plans they had for Ayodhya. My stance was that, while being fully loyal to the government, I could not be party to arrangements which would go contrary to the Supreme Court's directions on the subject or even the State Government's declared commitment to ensure the security of the shrine. Be that as it may, it was a case of State Government gradually losing its confidence in me. Subsequently, when I was given marching orders by Kalyan Singh on September 30, 1992, it was apparent that my professional attitude in the Ayodhya controversy had contributed in no small measure to my ouster.

In handling the Ayodhya issue, there were officers, who stood by me and there were officers, who were hobnobbing with the religious zealots. I would like to make a special mention of Dharam Vir Mehta, Inspector General, who was steadfastly loyal and thoroughly professional. Another Inspector General, who, thanks to Peter's Principle, managed to become DGP of a state, was a black sheep, passing on the details of discussions at the Police Headquarters to the political masters.

Terrorism

Terrorism in the terai area of UP was partly a spillover of terrorism of the Punjab and partly a reaction to the highhanded treatment meted out to the Sikh peasantry by a corrupt administration. In Punjab, *Operation Rakshak* had been launched by the security forces and, as a result, many terrorists fled from Punjab and sought shelter elsewhere. Terai had a sizeable Sikh population and was, therefore, considered a safe sanctuary. There were about ten terrorist outfits active in the terai area in the second half of 1991. The three major gangs were those of Satnam Singh Cheema, a self-styled Lt. General of Bhindranwala Tiger Force of Khalistan (BTFK), Balwinder Singh and Vichitra Singh/Swarn Singh. All of them carried assault rifles and had general purpose machine guns.

I found to my consternation that the state police was neither mentally nor physically prepared to meet the challenge. Terrorism was considered something beyond their capabilities. With the experience of Punjab and Assam behind me, I chalked out a comprehensive plan to deal with terrorism. Its salient features were:

— training the subordinate ranks in anti-terrorist techniques;
— equipping the force with sophisticated weapons;
— enhancing their mobility;
— improving their communications;
— providing additional manpower at police stations and establishing more police stations/outposts in affected areas;
— intensifying vigil along the Nepal border, and;
— raising two Task Force Battalions for the specific purpose of combating terrorism.

I must acknowledge that I got full cooperation from the government in implementing the above plan. Handpicked officers were posted in the districts affected by terrorism. These officers gave an excellent account of themselves. The force also rose to the occasion and, within a matter of about four to six months, started chasing the terrorists. Several important terrorist leaders were accounted for. These included Balwindar Singh alias Binda, self-styled Lt. Gen. of the Khalistan Commando Force, who was killed in Nainital on December 17, 1991, Satnam Singh alias Satta, who was annihilated in Dehradun on March 31, 1992, and Yadvendra Singh alias Yadu, self-styled Lt. Gen. of the Bhindranwala Tiger Force of Khalistan, who was shot down in an encounter in Nainital on May 4/5, 1992. A huge quantity of arms and ammunition were recovered from their possession. It was recognised by the BSF top brass that the PAC battalions operating in the terai were as effective as the BSF contingents.

My visit to the Nanakmata Gurudwara in Nainital district on September 8, 1991 was, in this context, a landmark event. I had been invited by the Gurudwara Prabandhak Committee and, in spite of government's advice to the contrary, decided to visit the Gurudwara. Nanakmata was looked upon as UP's Golden Temple and was frequented by terrorists. The police made comprehensive arrangements for my security, but once I entered the shrine I was surprised to see a gathering of about 15,000 Sikhs which, I was later told, had a good sprinkling of terrorists. I spoke to the gathering for about forty minutes, impressing upon them that they shall get justice from the police, that there would be no excesses, that the TADA cases shall be reviewed, but that terrorism shall not be tolerated and that those who had taken up arms shall be dealt with very severely. I reminded the Sikhs of their contribution to building up the Indian nation and exhorted them to join the mainstream. The correspondent of *Sunday Mail*, in an interview which was published on October 6, 1991 asked me: "You went to Nanakmata gurudwara recently. Don't you think you risked your neck as well as that of the government by going there?" My reply was: "I would rather take the risk. I would even go to hell if it means improving the situation in the terrorist-infested areas". The Sikh population realised that they could now expect a fair deal from the police. As Daljeet Singh Mann, Vice President of the UP Sikh Pratinidhi Board, said, "the Sikhs have full faith in the announcements of Prakash Singh because he fulfils the promises made". (*India Today*, Hindi edition, April 15, 1993). There was gradually a sea change in the situation.

My experience of different states including Assam, UP and the BSF convinced me that the force that we have is absolutely first class. The human material is second to none. How much they deliver, how much commitment and dedication they show depends entirely on the leadership – the extent to which it is able to inspire them, motivate them and get the best out of them.

6

The Trick Works !

B. J. MISAR

Maharashtra has three distinct regions – Western Maharashtra, Marathwada and Vidharbha. The people of Marathwada are supposed to be most docile. It was at one stage part of the Nizam's kingdom. The authority of the rulers was accepted meekly. This region has also produced a number of saints of Maharashtra. Everybody was surprised when the renaming of Marathwada University as Dr. Babasaheb Ambedkar University led to sudden and widespread riots in all the districts of Marathwada. Though all the MLAs had agreed to the renaming – the move had to be suspended. It was agreed to by the government that it would suspend the move for one year. The opposition on its part agreed to suspend the agitation for the same period. Unfortunately, no agreed solution emerged in this period. The opposition, therefore, resolved to revive the agitation, exactly after one year. I received orders of posting as DIG, Aurangabad range, three days prior to this dead line. I felt like sitting on top of a volcano, which may erupt any time !

The issue was highly emotive. People were sharply divided into two camps – pro- and anti-Namantar. The RPI supported the agitation. The other political parties also felt that it was a progressive move and should get them the dalit votes. The majority of the people of Marathwada were, however, deadly opposed to the change of the name – Namantar as they called it. My ex-boss, a retired IPS officer, was a leading member of the anti-Namantar camp !

The pro-Namantar groups decided to organise a Long March to Aurangabad – on the lines of Mao's famous Long March. They expected about two lakhs of volunteers from various districts to converge at Aurangabad and change the name of the university – as a *satyagraha*. Shri Sharad Pawar was the Chief Minister of a coalition government with thin majority. He was worried that the Maratha community from which he drew support may desert him if he supported the Long March. If he opposed the Long March, the dalits would desert him. Mrs. Indira Gandhi may supersede his government if there was repetition of violence against the weaker sections. My DG was a revolutionary. He was imprisoned during the freedom struggle. He was totally in favour of the renaming even at the cost of widespread violence. My predecessor DIG, in whose term the earlier riots erupted, was superseded for "weak leadership".

The anti-Namantar lobby had its own plans. They had realised that the police can control riots in cities much better than sporadic violence in the villages. They decided to give a call of schools and colleges bandh on the eve of the Long March. About one lakh volunteers would physically protect the university. Ten thousand women would lie prostate on the route of the Long March to block it. If any woman was touched by the marchers or the police – it would lead to violence. The most diabolical plan was to burn the huts of the dalits in the villages and break their bones.

I started sending my situation appreciation reports four months in advance. I made it clear that the Long March will not be permitted in my range. I requested the government to stop the Long March in the districts of origin and transit. There was no response till about a week prior to the deadline. The Home Secretary and the DGP came to Aurangabad. The meeting of DMs and SPs lasted for nine hours. The DGP insisted on permitting the Long March. The Divisional Commissioner and myself were adamant. The Home Secretary spoke to the CM and told him that widespread violence and bloodshed was inevitable if large numbers were allowed to gather at

Aurangabad. CM reluctantly agreed to stopping the Long March. The DGP was furious with me.

Our main problem was the villages. How to prevent violence in thousands of villages? We had started enquiries as to why the earlier riots could not be controlled. The experienced loyal staff, and even retired policemen were taken into confidence. They told us that most of the violence was committed by young college students. They were led by the sons of the Kulaks. Marathas held most of the seats of powers in panchayats, cooperative banks, zilla parishad and the like. If the sons of these leaders were arrested, pressure developed for their release. Since they could not be touched, the others led by them also got immunity. Their advice was – shake the chairs of the fathers ! Any threat to their seat of power would make them control their sons.

The problem boiled down to linking the suspension of the local body office bearers to violence. The Gram Panchayat Act, the Zilla Parishad Act provided suspension of the members for commission of any offence. Section 41 of the CrPC empowers the government to saddle anybody with the responsibility of reporting violence or crime to the police station. The Collector has the powers of suspension. A strategy emerged out of these otherwise unconnected pieces.

We drafted a Government Resolution saddling various elected bodies with responsibility of reporting violence in their respective areas to the police station. This draft in English was widely circulated to all the elected bodies. No Hindi or Marathi version was circulated to all the elected bodies. As was expected, the public leaders could not follow the legal jargon. They approached the local police and revenue officers for advice. The officers were already briefed. They told the leaders that in the event of violence in their areas, the non-dalit members would be suspended. The Collector would personally make enquiries. They may be given their seat if found innocent, for the remaining period of their term. In case the enquiries take long time, as they usually do, their term may expire before their release from suspension, which in reality would mean losing the hard won seat and suffer the rule by the dalit members till next election.

The solution was also found out jointly by the local leaders and the local officials. Ensure that there is no violence in your area. Ensure that your sons are kept locked up in the house for the period of the Long March. The magic worked. Some fourteen hundred public meetings were held by these leaders in the villages. They declared that despite their strong views on Namantar – protection of dalits was a point of honour for them ! They would provide them shelter in their own houses and *wadas*. Touching of a single Harijan even by the little finger would mean loss of face for them !

The draft government resolution remained a draft till the end. It was not even submitted to the government for approval. There was apprehension in our mind that government may not after all approve it. The local leaders, however, wanted to take no chances. Who would bother whether a snake is poisonous or non-poisonous? The Central Government had deputed a Secretary to ascertain the number of villages in which dalits apprehended riots. The Secretary was amazed that barring 36 villages, dalits did not insist on police pickets. They had more faith in the local leaders. When the Sarpanch swears that there would be no violence – there would be no violence. They turned out to be right. There was no violence in the villages – a complete contrast to the scene when Namantar was first attempted.

At the other end, the morchas were intercepted at various places. The ultimate number to reach Aurangabad was less than five thousand. There was some commotion at one place. Tear gas was used. A press reporter thought that he heard gun shots. He rushed the information. At Nagpur, a parallel morcha was on. It got emotive. In police firing, two persons got killed !

The real issue in the city was different. If the pro- and anti-Namantarwadis were to clash even in small groups, a chain reaction would have set in. The problem was to keep the anti-Namantarwadis cool. We had assured them repeatedly that Namantar would be allowed only if the Assembly passed a Bill to that effect. However, their faith in the government was shaky. My ex-boss approached the local SP. He asked him bluntly whether we were playing a double game. The MLAs had already passed a resolution agreeing to Namantar. The Government may permit the morcha to reach the university. They may forcibly change the name – once Dr. Babasaheb Ambedkar's name appeared on the arch at university entrance, it would remain so for sentimental reasons. The SP could convince the ex-boss citing some reasons.

The morcha had commenced at Nagpur. Prof. Jogendra Kawade announced that the morcha would replace the name at the university. We immediately registered an offence against him at Aurangabad under Section 117 IPC. This section, makes inciting ten or more persons to commit violence or any offence even peacefully, a cognisable offence. Unlike Section 153 (A), no government sanction is necessary. Whether persons actually got instigated or not is immaterial. This section acts against the instigating leader not against the instigated followers. It proved that we were not treating the events lightly.

My ex-boss had already come to know of the discussions in the nine-hour meeting held by the Home Secretary. However, what convinced him most was our action against all breaking the law, irrespective of their political affiliation, or the feelings of the ruling party. The ruling party desired that the provocative speeches of the dalit leaders hurting the religious feelings of the Hindus be ignored. The dalit Panthers used to misbehave in public. The common grazing lands in the villages were encroached upon by the Harijans. Ruling party desired that we would adopt a soft attitude. We were, however, very firm. Even the minute infringement of law was dealt with very firmly. I had learnt these lessons from my ex-boss himself. He had watched my actions as DIG very closely.

I appealed to the Anti-Namantar Committee to refrain from any confrontation. The administration would ensure the safety of the university. Law and law alone would change the name of the university. My ex-boss used his clout with the Namantar Virodhi Samiti. He himself had served as DIG, Aurangabad range when I was SP in Parabhani. His assurance was accepted by all. Direct confrontation between the rivals was avoided.

This helped us a lot. It was police versus the agitators and not pro- *versus* anti-Namantarwadis.

About three thousand Satyagrahis were detained for a day and let off. Only Kawade was arrested under Section 117 IPC. No stone pelting, no injuries. There was relief all-round. We felt happy as the mother feels after delivery. She forgets all the pangs of delivery when she holds the new born in arms. We got letters of appreciation. The dalit leaders met me and thanked the police for saving their lives and property. Government held a meeting of all the Secretaries. All the Secretaries were urged on to study the operations and identify the strong points. We also reflected calmly to identify the strong points.

1. Though people have a right to assemble peacefully without arms, large-scale gatherings when the rivals are worked up on emotive issues are dangerous.
2. Bans are naturally perceived as hostile steps by the agitators. Motives are alleged. Police are seen as mere agents of the ruling political party. We must prove by our conduct that ruling political party and the administration are different and have their own agenda.
3. Indian villagers, despite their lack of formal education, are very wise. Subordinate police officers know the realities a lot better than their seniors. Arrogance of authority snaps our communications with them.
4. Macaulay's laws are a marvel, IPC, CrPC can give us unlimited powers. However, law is always to be found and used imaginatively.
5. Long-term preventive strategy pays. The more you sweat in peace, the less you bleed in war.
6. The full responsibility must always rest with the local officers. There is no point in taking shelter behind the orders or advise of the superiors or the ruling party.
7. Police must always retain the confidence not only of the majority, but of every faction of the society. If they do justice to all, peace will look after itself.

Years after retirement, I read an article on Kashmir issue in the *Times of India*. It was by Shri Ved Marwah. He said that as long as the Kashmir policeman behaved as policemen, none can take away Kashmir from us. At first, I considered this to be an extreme statement. However, as I read the whole article I was convinced that it was a true statement. The reasoning was found in *Mahabharata*. This is something, which every policeman and every politician should know.

In *Shanti Parva*, Bhishma explains the birth, life and death of the State. Human society is always full of conflicts between individuals and groups. Such conflicts shall never end ! How prophetic ! He further adds that such conflicts do not harm the society ! The king and rulers have to manage the conflicts. They have to remember that all are children of God. God does not tolerate harm to any of his children. If the rulers lose confidence of even a single faction, they lose their kingdom. God simply withdraws the power entrusted to them. In case the rulers misuse the powers against the weaker sections, he destroys them at the hands of these very persons. This is how Kauravas got destroyed at the hands of the Pandavas.

Power equations are very deceptive. God can change them in a minute. He is the Supreme Master. We should never forget him. Supporting the weak against the mighty is always a difficult task. However, we, the police, are trustees for the weak, appointed by the God. We should not chicken out in facing difficulties. His help will come from nowhere. He will solve all the difficulties. He is so large hearted that he would even permit you to hog all the credit for yourself !

7

Some Reminiscences

B.R. KALYANPURKAR

When I was asked to contribute an article, narrating one of my unique experiences as a law enforcement officer, to a collection of reflections and reminiscences of a number of distinguished police officers in the form of a book, which is intended to be of practical use to serving officers, I hesitated for three reasons. Firstly, unlike many of my colleagues in the service, I have not had a distinguished career. In fact, the only time my name ever appeared in the press in my entire career was not for anything that I had done, but because the press had been critical of "police atrocities" in dealing with the states re-organisation riots in Ahmedabad in 1956, and my DIG insisted that my picture with a bandaged head and blood-soaked shirt should be released to the press to show that the police had also been at the receiving end of mob violence. Secondly, any retired officer writing for the benefit of serving officers would be accused of pontificating. Thirdly, I have not had any unique experiences. My experiences have been those of any ordinary police officer. But every ordinary police officer has a large number of interesting experiences, however trivial, and serving officers may like to read about them though they may not be of any practical use to them. I myself have enjoyed, and sometimes benefited from, reading books written by retired and serving officers. So I have decided that there is no harm in penning some of my experiences and leaving it to the editor to decide whether my contribution should be included in the book. I will write about some trivial but interesting experiences which left me either personally satisfied or frustrated or embarrassed or proud.

I served in the junior scale as a Sub-Divisional Police Officer for full five years, and was required to personally supervise the investigation of all serious crimes and to take over for personal investigation at least ten cases every year. One of the earliest cases of murder investigated by me was in a small village in Jalgaon district in Maharashtra. A farmer in his late forties lived with his wife, his twenty-year old son and the son's sixteen-year old wife. The father was a virile tyrant, who repeatedly forced himself on his young daughter-in-law, and neither she, nor his wife or son, dared to protest or to complain to anyone. After some months of this, the son could not take it any more, and one night when the father was asleep at home on his *charpai*, the son killed him with a blow of an axe on his head. The next morning the inmates informed the neighbours that they had found the father dead, presumably killed by some unknown intruder. The Sub-Inspector was informed and, on going to the village, found no signs of anyone having broken into the house. When I reached the village, I found the Sub-Inspector hectoring and abusing the young son. I took over the investigation and questioned the son, speaking to him softly and addressing him, as was my wont, in the honorific second person plural. After some time, he came out with the whole story and produced the murder weapon from a shallow dry well, where he had concealed it. The investigation was simple, but I was in a dilemma when I chargesheeted him for the offence of murder. I felt that he was morally not guilty as he had taken the law in his own hands out of sheer helplessness, and the father had got what he deserved. My hands were tied by the letter of the law, and I felt most frustrated. Fortunately, his trial for murder came up before a very humane Sessions Judge, who interpreted the facts in such a way that he was able to give him a three years' sentence instead of a life sentence.

Another case of murder I was involved with much later, and equally frustrating for me, was when I was doing legal aid work as an advocate at the Supreme Court after my retirement. A widow was left with two sons, a house and a farm. She lived in her house with her elder son, who was married, and her younger son used to do temporary jobs away from their village and visit his home occasionally. The elder son ill-treated his mother, appropriated the house and farm and eventually beat up his mother and threw her out of her house, forcing her to seek shelter with distant relations in another village. When the younger brother returned home to visit his mother and brother, his elder brother told him he did not know where their mother was. On hearing what had happened from some neighbours, he quarrelled with his elder brother over his treatment of their mother. Blows were exchanged, and on the heat of the moment the younger brother picked up a farm implement lying in the house and hit the elder brother with it, killing him. The trial court held that it was a case of murder and sentenced the young man to life imprisonment. The conviction and sentence were upheld by the High Court. In a special leave petition I tried to persuade their Lordships in the Supreme Court that the accused had been gravely provoked on hearing that his mother had been beaten and thrown out of her house by his brother, and also that the accused had committed the homicide without premeditation in a sudden fight in the heat of passion upon a sudden quarrel. I was most frustrated when my petition was summarily dismissed.

I have had two very embarrassing experiences. My first priority in service was to acquire and retain a reputation for honesty, and in this I failed. In my first posting as Sub-Divisional Police Officer, as I did not want to utilise my orderlies for domestic work and did not want the hospitality of my subordinates, I engaged a cook, who used to go with me everywhere in my car on my tours and produce quick meals wherever I camped. A box in the boot of my car had pots and pans and provisions, but vegetables were bought locally for which I gave my cook money from time to time and he would account for the money spent. At one camp, where I was inspecting a police station, he fell ill, and though he was well enough to cook, he entrusted the shopping to a constable. When the constable tried to account for the money I had given, the account did not tally, and strangely he returned more change than he should have. When I confronted him with my calculation, he admitted he had taken things free from the Sub-Inspector, whose police station I was inspecting. I confronted the Sub-Inspector, who disclosed that my cook had also been doing the same thing. I was embarrassed that the Sub-Inspector must have thought that I had been living off him, and horrified at the thought that my cook may have done the same thing at other places during the few months he had been with me. I dismissed him on the spot, and started having my meals in restaurants, and if I had to go to small villages where there were no restaurants, I would carry a stock of bananas and bread with me to subsist on. My marriage later saved me from this Spartan diet. But my reputation in my first sub-division must have been tarnished by my cook.

I had another embarrassing moment when I was giving evidence in a Sessions Court in a murder case I had investigated in another posting. A land dispute between two families in a village had led to a clash between members of the two families, and some persons had been injured and one killed. In the first information report, the complainant had named several persons as accused, and the investigating officer had arrested all of them. When I reached the place and took over the investigation, I found that one of those arrested had not been involved in the clash at all and had been falsely implicated by the complainant, whose version was not corroborated by other witnesses. I, therefore, sent up the chargesheet only against all the other accused. The Sessions Judge, who was exceptional in that he did not have a particularly good reputation for integrity, could not believe that I could have left one of the named accused out of the chargesheet without taking any money. When I was giving evidence about my investigation, pointed questions were put to me suggesting that something undesirable and improper must have been done by me. When I came out of the court room, I was seething helplessly at the false aspersion.

I had some very satisfying experiences during my executive service. In 1995, Bhusawal was not communally as sensitive as it was in later years, but the Ganesh Chaturthi processions had potential for trouble. In the previous year, there had been minor clashes when the processionists carrying Ganpati idols for immersion had created a din outside the masjid at the time of namaz. There was a suggestion that the traditional route of the procession should be changed. My advice was that this would not be necessary, and I undertook to regulate the procession on the traditional route and ensure that there would be no trouble. I persuaded the local Muslim leaders to put up with whatever din the processionists made before the time of namaz. I told the Hindu leaders that the procession carrying the Ganpati idols would not be a continuous one and would be required to pass the masjid before the time of namaz. Accordingly, I made arrangements that each group carrying an idol would be separated from the next group before it arrived in the vicinity of the masjid. The first group was then physically escorted with a lot of pushing and shoving by the policemen led by an Inspector and me, while the road was blocked for the subsequent groups. After the first group had passed beyond the masjid, we similarly escorted the second group. Each group tried deliberately to linger as long as possible in front of the masjid and the volume of their slogans reached a crescendo. By sheer physical effort of pushing we managed to see all the groups pass beyond the masjid before the time of namaz. The peaceful passing off of the event gave me immense satisfaction.

In 1955, a notorious armed gang of dacoits was active in both the Eastern and Western sub-divisions of Banaskantha district of Gujarat and also in the adjoining Sirohi district of Rajasthan. When I took charge of the Eastern sub-division, I used to play hockey with the men of the armed police posted at the district headquarters, and got to know and trust some of the good players, who were also good marksmen. I left instructions that as soon as any report of an armed dacoity was received, the jeep allotted to me should collect a head-constable and three constables picked by me from among the hockey players, and when they drew rifles from the armoury, they should draw an extra one for me, and come and fetch me. One night, the gang of dacoits struck at a village at the foot of the Aravali Hills which separated Banaskantha from Sirohi district. On receiving the information, my men and I drove to the village arriving there at dawn. Leaving the local Sub-Inspector to do the paper work, I walked out of the village with my four armed men and a tracker from the village to follow the tracks of the dacoits which led us to the Aravali Hills and were then lost. The hill range was much smaller than the adjoining Mount Abu, and was strewn with large rocks and bushes. Searching for the gang of armed dacoits on that hill range was like looking for a needle in a haystack. It was also a little foolhardy as the dacoits could have spotted us first from behind the rocks or bushes, and we could initially have been an easy target. But we were better armed and better trained and physically fit, so it was an even contest. We combed the hill range without rest from dawn to dusk with only our water bottles for sustenance, without any success. But this was the best preventive action I could have taken, for the gang may have seen us or come to know about our immediate combing operation. No more armed dacoities were reported in my sub-division for the rest of my posting there, and this was very satisfying for me as the gang continued to strike in other areas.

Finally, I come to an incident which made me proud. I had left the executive police and had been working in an intelligence agency. For some years, I was responsible for recruiting and training officers joining the agency in ranks equivalent to Sub-Inspector and Assistant Sub-Inspector. When I was later posted to Shillong in the North-East and covered five states including some with problems of insurgency, many of the officers, I had come in close touch with as trainees, were posted in that region at remote posts in areas considered unsafe. The strength of a post were one SI and one ASI. Our officers at these posts were unarmed as a matter of policy. In one remote post in Mizoram, which was a two days' march from the headquarters at Aizawl, when the SI was away on leave, the ASI was shot dead by the underground when he had gone to meet a contact. When I drove from Shillong to Aizawl, the body was still on its way to Aizawl from the post. I went to call on the Lt. Governor and on IGP of Mizoram. Both of them offered their condolences and predicted that any one transferred to that post in the vacancies of the deceased ASI and the SI who had completed his tenure at that post, would wriggle out of the posting. The body arrived during the night, and next morning I held a condolence meeting of all our officers posted at Aizawl. After my memorial speech, I announced that for the filling up of the vacancies caused at the post, only those who volunteered would be posted. Immediately one SI and one ASI stepped forward and said they were ready to go to that post. I have never felt so proud or been so deeply moved in the course of my service.

8

Looking Back

D.K. ARYA

The course of life is changed sometimes by a seemingly insignificant incident. I recount my own experience. An average undergraduate student of humanities, without a clear aim, mentor, guide or a role model, I was muddling through my studies. The future was far distant and the present was pleasant. Boast sparring among friends was a favourite pastime and one-up-manship was the name of the game. Nainital, my hometown, was a beautiful place of pristine beauty in the early fifties and the summers were glorious. Thousands thronged 'our' Mall and the ritualistic evening strolls were exhilarating. Strolling with a close friend I secretly envied, we were animatedly airing our favourite fantasies. Each one of us had our future well chalked out. He, a tall, athletic and talented person, had set his sights on becoming an IPS officer. To be one-up-on him, I wanted to join the elite 'ICS'. This rather impassioned discussion on the virtues, powers and authorities of respective dream services would have continued but for a gentle tap on my shoulder. It was a distinguished looking elderly gentleman. With an amused but benign smile on his face, he apologised for overhearing us. He gently reminded me that ICS was history and IAS was the successor service and that I should better make certain my facts before I went out to realise my dreams. Jolted out of my fantasies, I felt so stupid and ashamed that I wanted to jump into the lake ! Those words have always been a beacon for me and gave me the wisdom to keep my feet on terra firma. I am eternally grateful to that unknown benefactor who, by his gentle reminder, changed the course of my life, gave me direction and encouraged me to pursue a real objective and not a fantasy.

It has been a long and eventful, albeit chequered service career and there are events one remembers but not many that one would care to recount. I have great faith in our constitutional institutions. The Supreme Court, the EC, the CAG, the UPSC, to name a few. There are reasons for it. I vividly remember the day I appeared for my IPS interview in February 1960. As an unsure, shy and diffident 22 year old from the hills, I was uneasy and nervous in a borrowed suit. Confronting me were five formidable looking members of the Board. If I recollect correctly, Mr. Hasan Jaheer was heading the Board. Among the many 'extra curricular' activities, I had mentioned boxing in my childhood and trekking in my youth as my favourites. Pat came the query. Where had I learned boxing? I had studied in a government school and not in a reputed Convent of Nainital. Government schools did not provide boxing lessons. Without realising the implications, I told them that I had learned boxing in the nearby branch of a then officially 'out of favour' organisation. There were many searching follow up questions and I had a feeling that my responses made in transparent innocence had perhaps impressed the Board. When I was called to join the IPS, I knew whom to thank besides the God. The great institution called UPSC continues to be above political considerations and still upholds the values set for it by our Constitution makers.

While undergoing training in Abu, I was allotted to MP cadre. It did not mean much to me as all I had known of Madhya Pradesh was what I had read while preparing for general knowledge paper. For me, it was the back of beyond. One day I received a parcel containing MP Police Regulation with a DO letter from (Late) Shri R.N. Nagu, the DIG Administration. I still have the letter which had warmly welcomed me to the Cadre and exhorted me to familiarise myself with the Police Regulation and that it would stand me in good stead in my career. I was overwhelmed by the warmth of the welcome and ever since have felt proud of belonging to MP cadre.

(Late) Shri P.R. Rajgopal was my DIG Range. Prakash Naidu and I went to Jabalpur for our Departmentals. We called on him and were invited to dinner. His wife served us dinner and with motherly warmth kept heaping the delightful vegetarian dishes on our plates till we were ready to burst. We had planned to take a rickshaw to a movie and then return to the Mess. Shri Rajgopal took out his personal car and insisted on driving us to the cinema hall. I have the sweetest of memories of my ASP days where the seniors took great care to be mentor, teacher and guide, and treated young ASPs like younger brothers. May be I was lucky to have mentors like Shri K.S. Dhillon, Shri Rajgopal, Shri Nagu, Shri Rustamji and many others. That MP cadre is a great fraternity, full of camaraderie, was amply demonstrated by the fabulous Retired Officers', Seminar held in Bhopal in the first week of March, 2002. A large number of retired officers from far and wide came to meet and rejoice. I am sure all of us felt proud of belonging to MP cadre.

In 1962-63, I was ASP Gwalior and Sector Officer, Anti-Dacoity Operations in Behat circle. Late Ganga Sewak Trivedi, who had risen from the rank of a constable, was DSP CID. A man endowed with photographic memory, great wit and dazzling brilliance, he was a past master in police procedure and *peshbandi*. He had a mischievous twinkle in his eyes and an insolent grin that could put one in one's place. He once asked me to keep in readiness to arrest two dreaded dacoits, who would be coming to buy ammunition from a contact in Gwalior. He did not tell me where or when. I was fed encouraging information every hour or two. Shivering in intense Gwalior cold, I sat like a fool in my jeep for the entire night to be told in the morning that the buyers had smelled a trap and that the operation was over. When I told of my ordeal to the SP, who himself was an old campaigner, I was advised to always verify the reliability of the informer before jumping to comply. He told me to strike a balance between *josh* and *durusti*. Much later, when I was on deputation, I met Ganga Sewak and asked about the failed operation. The mischievous glint in eyes was back and in his inimitably oblique way it was conveyed to me that my overzealousness needed to be trimmed lest I got into trouble. I do not think I would have learnt a lesson if someone had given me a straight lecture on temperance.

In Gwalior, I learnt another lesson for life. As Sector Officer AD Operations in Behat sector, I used to visit villages for collection of intelligence about movement of gangs and their harbourers, suppliers of food and information to them. A probationary SI from Behat PS would accompany me. We asked questions, berated villagers, were harsh with them and dispensed rough and ready justice if no truthful or satisfactory answer to our queries was forthcoming. My regular companion was transferred out and another PSI was assigned to me. We visited a notorious village and called the Sarpanch and a few known harbourers. The Sarpanch saw a different SI with me and queried me about the previous one. I told him that he had been transferred out. On this the Sarpanch tut-tutted, called him an effective officer and lamented about his transfer. I was surprised and commented that the said PSI had used invectives and resorted to 'shoe beating' and wondered how and why they rated him as a good officer. His reply made good sense. For him the PSI was a 'hakim' and had every right to take punitive action against naughty men and added that though he (PSI) beat them with shoes but never on the head, only on the back. Their dignity was not lowered. Only physical punishment was given which was their fate and they deserved. I have always kept that lesson in mind. Never to humiliate or degrade any one and never add insult to injury.

The '62 war was on and news of the debacle was slowly filtering in. There was widespread fear that the Chinese may occupy large chunks of our territory across the Himalayas. The Kumaoni in me was in anguish. My land was in grave danger and I was wasting my life running after petty dacoits. I shot off a letter to the IG (Shri Rustamji) offering to go anywhere to fight the Chinese. I was interviewed by Shri B.N. Mullick, the DIB, was accepted and was seconded to ITBP, where I served for eleven straight years. Those were the days of learning Chinese methods of guerrilla warfare, stay behind, sabotage, improvisation, living off the land, 'long marches' etc. We, of the

Second Battalion, moved from Chakrata to Kalsi after completing very gruelling and intensive 'unconventional warfare' training. Late Sardar Balbir Singh, our IG, wanted to test our physical fitness and endurance and the Battalion was ordered to march from Kalsi (near Chakrata) to Rai (near Sonepat). As others were not available(?) to march, I being the Adjutant and Training Officer, it fell on me to lead the column. It was May 12, 1964, and we marched through Dehradun, Roorkee, Saharanpur, Meerut, Baghpat and wade through Yamuna to Rai. Temperature during day time soared to 44-45°C. It was an over 900 men column stretching for about a mile in length. I walked the entire 230 odd miles with the men in 9 days averaging about 29 miles a day with just one day of rest in between. How we did it I do not care to remember. Most of the time we were in a trance. There were two companies of Tibetans and rest of the troops were all hill men. How we all suffered ! Tossing and unable to sleep under the shade of mango and leechi trees in that scorching heat. How we walked (sleep walk !) through the night nobody other than us and our God knows. Many of us were bleeding through various orifices of the body. Tibetans hallucinated and screamed. It was a nine-day nightmare. There were many casualties. What a great bunch of mules we were and almost 90 per cent of us reached Rai in one piece and no one died ! No one turned insane ! It sounds simple today but as the leader (just 4 years service) I marched with the men, receed the next stop, found water, briefed leaders every evening before the march, took roll call at the halt point, took stock of weapons and equipments, saw to food and water and looked after the health of men. It was a great lesson in managing men and their (and mine) morale. I lost 7 kg. weight in 9 days. While we all took great pride in making the march in time, what riled us most was that everyone who met us on the road thought that we were under some punishment for mutiny !

Late Shri B.N. Mullick was an acerbic, acidic, ascetic man possessing formidable personality, great will power and vision. We were in awe of him. He was too critical of the army logistics tail and did not want us to ape the army. His ideal was the Chinese way of fighting with the minimum logistical burden.

He hated tinned stuff and would prefer 'langar' food to the one cooked in a well stocked Mess. I was then building the Second Bn Hqrs. Nucleus at Gwaldam. Shri Mullick dropped in to see us and was received by Shri D.V.L.N. Ramakrishna Rao and myself. We took him to the Forest Rest House where I was putting up. Over a cup of tea he heard my report on the progress of construction work. He was in a good mood. Short distance away he saw the tents of our pioneer section and other workingmen. Pointing out to a goat tethered to a tent rope he asked me what it was. Obviously, it was a goat but I thought he wanted to know what was it for. I instinctively replied that it was "meat on hoof" and realised that I had put my foot in my mouth. He exploded and let me have the full measure of his wrath. 'You ape the army without acquiring its capabilities', he glowered at me. Meat on hoof is now no more in my dictionary. Having spent his wrath on us, he left and we took a sigh of relief. We had barely settled down to a relaxed cup of tea, his helicopter returned.

A dense fog had prevented his departure. We would have to endure him for the night. He insisted for the 'langar' food and we ate it in morbid silence. He had not forgiven us (me) for the meat on hoof fiasco. Our 'temporary mess waiter' would not consider the dinner complete without the 'sweet dish'. He, using his initiative, opened a can of tinned apricots, which we had saved from our Chakrata army rations. Shri Mullick turned red in rage. Army rations again! I have never been on the receiving end of such tongue lashing in my life. We both cried. A goat is a goat and tinned fruit was simply army ration. Why such fuss !

One winter afternoon, when I was busy supervising construction work, I was handed over a 'crash' message from ITBP Hqrs., directing me to see the IG at 11.00 hrs. the next morning barely 18 hours later. It did not occur to me to ask for a postponement and rushed to comply. I was well trained in operational preparedness and packed necessary travel requirements and uniform and moved on to keep my appointment. The driver, on deputation from Gujarat Police, misjudged an oncoming truck near Kausani and the resultant accident disabled the jeep but we both were uninjured. I forced the quaking truck driver to drive me back to Gwaldam. He brought me to Garud, 13 miles short of Gwaldam and there his truck died on me. It did not revive despite my threats of dire consequences. In sheer desperation, I trekked about 8 miles by foot-trail in semi-darkness to Gwaldam, picked another jeep, drove recklessly the whole night and reached Delhi in the morning, covering a distance of about 400 km., almost half of which was hill section. I freshened up, changed into uniform and proudly presented myself before the AIG (Senapaty?), just in time for the appointment. After an interminable wait for over one hour, I was told that the IG would see me at 12.00 hrs. the next day as he was busy ! Obviously, I had not really learnt the Ganga Sewak lesson well. In retrospect, I realise that a command may become a matter of life or death for a junior officer, it may not be of much concern to a senior officer. Different perspectives for different ranks ! However, to complete the narrative, I met the IG at the appointed time, 24 hours later. He wanted me to plan a march of the Second Bn. from Rai to Gwaldam—500 kms away—with me as the leader. I told him of my experience and the effect on the morale of men measuring the road on foot when buses and trucks were whizzing past carrying people. Walking in the hills was different, I told him. He countered with a suggestion that we should march cross country. The usual impediments like rivers Ganga, Jamuna, Ramganga, Kosi, etc., should be crossed by using improvised river crossing methods. He advised me to avoid roads, draw a straight line between Rai and Gwaldam and march on a compass bearing ! He brushed aside all my arguments. Thankfully, I was temporarily attached to Rai Training Centre and escaped the ordeal.

Early 1968, the IG called me to Delhi to raise an indigenous martial band. This was to replace the western brass and pipe bands. Great patriotic idea. Local colour. Reminiscent of India's golden period. I had no clue and no one in the ITBP Hqrs. could guide me how to go about it. I met Acharya Bruhaspati, Akashvani's Indian classical music expert, and had a long chat with him. At the end of which, he appeared amused and I was confused. He advised me to meet Anil Biswas, the great composer, who also was with Akashvani. He, too, was amused but gave me a patient hearing and suggested inclusion of many traditional martial instruments but could not tell me where or how to get them. I could not enthuse him to compose martial music or marching tunes. I met bandmasters of Army and Navy bands, who were sceptical but sympathetic and offered to suggest good retired or retiring bandsmen for our project. No guidance was forthcoming from them. I then met in Lucknow, Captain Ram Singh, associate of Netaji Subhash Chandra Bose, and the legendary INA bandmaster credited with the famous *kadam kadam badaye ja, khushi ke geet gaye ja*. After a few lengthy sessions with him, I was able to crystallise my ideas. Ex-army bandsmen, local artists and 'barat' bandwalas were recruited. Instruments were bought, borrowed, begged or commandeered through battalions of border areas. An ensemble consisting of strange, uncoordinated but martial looking instruments was put together. We valiantly tried to develop some 'shuffling' tunes. I thought we had devoted enough time on it and wanted the DG (he had become DG Security by then) to have a look at it and guide us to the next stage. A demonstration was put up at ITBP camp in Tigri. All ITBP and IB top brass were there. After inspecting those exotic instruments, the VIPs stood close in front of the band. The bandmaster waved his baton and the screeching, ear drum splitting sounds that emanated made the crowd run for cover. That was the day of the birth and demise of an idea.

How I came back to my state is a different story, but the few districts that I commanded as SP were the stages of my virtually re-learning police work. Later in 1977 (after emergency was over) as SP, Mandsaur, I could not cope with the expectations of the new regime, specially of the Chief Minister, whose constituency it was, and his cronies. I would not accommodate their overt and covert hints and pernicious pressure. The 11 straight years on deputation had taught me how not to bend backwards. The IG (state Police Chief) remarked that my dossier spoke volumes about my talents as a trainer and that I would very do well as Commandant of a training battalion. Shortly thereafter, I was earmarked for state to state deputation to Mizoram as DIG. Without a word, I went and joined there. Mizoram was then reeling under severe insurgency. During the 'outsiders out' violent movement in June 1979, the Aizawl Collectorate was 'gheraoed' and information was available that it may be set on fire. The SP was on leave, I being the senior most police officer present, faced determined demonstrators. We had CRPF in support. All negotiations having failed, we were about to warn the demonstrators to disperse when stones started to rain on us. A large powerfully hurled stone struck my shoulder and I fell. The DSP in panic asked CRPF to use force to disperse the demonstrators. And local police and CRPF let the demonstrators have it. Legs were broken and heads were split. Most injured were young girls and women, who had been put in front as shields by the demonstrators. Fortunately, I was wearing a helmet but no other defensive equipment. In retrospect, I realise that had I been wearing proper defensive equipments, I would not have been hurt and the resultant excessive force used by police against vulnerable women and children could have been avoided.

In 1985, when I was DIG in ITBP, Shri M.C. Misra, DG, BSF, asked me to take over as Director, BSF Academy, Tekanpur. I could never say no to him despite serious problems of my children's education and took over in February, 1986. The Academy was an army-oriented institution as all its previous Directors had been army officers. How I made attitudinal adjustments is another story. Came severe summers of '86 and 3000 strong BSF schools population was let loose in Tekanpur. Vandalism, eve-teasing, street fighting, theft of two and four wheelers, forcible rides on passing vehicles, and general delinquent behaviour became a daily norm. It became our problem. The exuberance had to be channelled and diverted towards positive and healthy behaviour. We organised children's summer camps and hired good coaches from the Laxmibai College of Physical Education for coaching in cricket, basket ball, hockey, swimming, tennis and used our own instructors to teach karate, judo, shooting, horse riding, battle craft, nature study, photography, etc. Delinquent behaviour was instantly replaced by healthy competition, camaraderie and friendship among children of different classes of society. To me, it was a successful experiment and a worthy welfare measure.

I took over as BSF DG in early 1994. Kashmir scenario was bleak, specially after the Bijbehra aberration in October '93. Damage control exercise was on and the morale of troops needed perking up. I persuaded Justice Rangnath Misra, Chairman, NHRC and other members of the Commission to see for themselves the conditions under which the BSF troops were working. He was distressed to witness the level of danger the men were exposed to and the unbearable stress and pressure the men were working under. The visit helped correct the perspective of NHRC towards BSF in Kashmir. In a related trip to Srinagar in severe winter, I went on a round of various posts. I met a 20 year old 'Prahari' standing guard on a bridge as the dawn was breaking. It was bitterly cold and the wind chill factor was enough to freeze anyone's bone marrow. It was his first ever posting and he had recently married. He looked frightened because he was, too, exposed and miserable because he was too cold. We got to chatting and I asked him if he was okay and if I could be of any help to him. All that he came out with after a lot of goading was that the bitter cold on the bridge drove him insane. He would not sit inside the 'morcha' and draw warmth from the brazier. The stoicism, the grit and the sense of duty demonstrated by the man in such adverse conditions filled me with great pride. I do not know if he survived his tenure in Srinagar. We had lost more than 500 men in Kashmir and thousands were maimed and injured. I dreaded to go to the Army Base Hospital in Srinagar because I could not face men paralysed, disfigured and maimed. Their wives, parents, or relatives wrote letters asking for their welfare. Many men, who were disfigured or paralysed, beseeched us not to disclose their true condition to their families. A visit to Kashmir was always a heart rending experience.

We wanted to revive the 'Welfare Melas', which had given good exposure to BSF. In preparation, we invited families and widows for an interaction. My wife and I were appalled to see the number of very young widows, some of whom were even carrying infants in their lap. We wondered if we could get them to agree to remarry. My wife asked them their problems which were many including deprivation by their in-laws of the money received by them from the government, maltreatment, sexual harassment, etc. She then broached the subject of their remarriage to gauge their reaction. Furtively, looking at each other, they declined. We knew that widow remarriage was still not acceptable in the rural community wherefrom a bulk of constabulary was drawn. Two-three weeks later, two widows met my wife in the welfare centre and expressed willingness to remarry. They had consulted their parents. Efforts began in right earnest to find willing grooms for them. The number of willing widows swelled to six. We did not want to go the 'Times Matrimonial' or to Professor Arora's Regarpura marriage bureau. We decided to exhort our BSF men to hold the hands of their fallen comrades' widows. I made emotional appeals to men during 'Sainik Sammelans' all over the borders. The men nobly responded and came forward. Officers and their wives worked hard at match making. The marriages were solemnised and the then Union Home Minister and his wife were there to bless. The Prime Minister received them and gave gifts and was gracious enough to make an appreciative mention of this genuine experiment in the Parliament. During my tenure, over 21 widows were remarried to BSF jawans and a trend was set. It was, to my mind, a great morale booster for the troops and a very satisfying contribution from both of us.

9

The Sikkim Saga

B.S. DAS

Sikkim was in serious trouble in April, 1973. The anti-Chogyal forces were up in arms demanding democratic rights based on 'one man, one vote'. The elections had been rigged putting the pro-Chogyal party, a Bhutia minority, in power. Clashes broke out and the Sikkim Government collapsed. Indian army was called in. The police was disarmed. Mobs had robbed the police stations of all weapons and wireless sets. The administration ceased to function.

I was called in by the Foreign Secretary, Kewal Singh on 8th April and asked to take over the Sikkim administration on 9th. My brief was to restore order, revive the Government, negotiate with the pro- and anti-Chogyal political parties, hold free elections and set up a new Government. I was designated as the Chief Executive.

Flown into Gangtok under strict security, I was welcomed by slogan shouting crowds demanding an end to the Chogyal's rule. Sikkim then was a Protectorate of India, governed by the Indo-Sikkim Treaty of 1950 under which the Maharaja (the Chogyal, a Tibetan title given to the ruler) governed Sikkim with foreign relations being under Delhi's representative, the Political Officer.

On 9th April, when I was flying out of Delhi, the national newspapers splashed the news of Sikkim take over with my name and photograph all over. The Chinese launched a vehement political attack on India's action. China claimed Sikkim as its territory. Its troops were right on Sikkim's border facing the Indian Army.

When I took over, I had no staff from India nor any para-military or intelligence support. I was totally on my own. The Indian Army was located at strategic places to guard but refused to take over any law and order duties unless accompanied by local Magistrates. The civil administration having collapsed, all civil servants were in hiding. When I went to call on the Chogyal on 10th April, he said to me:

"Mr. Das, Sikkim is not Goa that you have come to take over. We are an independent country with our own identity". Brave words indeed, but without any support.

The very first task was to restore law and order, make the civil administration functional and recover all looted firearms. I called two local Magistrates and went to the central point of the agitation where all roads were blocked. I had to show my strength. I had a meeting with the political leaders and assured them of restoring their legitimate political rights, consider their demands and then hold elections as per agreement as may be arrived at between all the political parties. For this, they had to give me full cooperation and allow the administration to function. They had lots of reservations but finally agreed.

On 12th April, the police was called back to duty. I then called a meeting of political leaders and asked them to surrender all looted weapons. Firstly, they denied the looting but then agreed to return if they were not prosecuted. The Police Commissioner, a senior IPS officer, refused to agree. I then called the Chief Secretary and between us, we overruled the Police Commissioner. I told the Commissioner that while I appreciated his view as a Police Officer, exigencies of the political factors needed some hard decisions. I took full responsibility for my decisions as head of the Government in spite of Chogyal's serious opposition. Within the stipulated time of 3 days, all weapons were quietly surrendered. With all these developments, offices opened and general life started returning to normalcy. By 16th April, I had managed to complete the first phase of my task. But the major issue remained—a political settlement.

Delhi was coming under lot of pressure internationally apart from China. India was out to swallow Sikkim. How could

India violate the Treaty ! Barring Soviet Union, I doubt if any other country was sympathetic. Even Soviet Union was advising Delhi to complete the political process at the earliest to prevent China from over reacting.

The political talks ran into trouble. There was no compromise on 'one man one vote'. The Chogyal and his supporting National Party refused to even discuss the issue. If they accepted this demand, they would lose power being in a hopeless minority. Meanwhile, I was facing many problems. The entire civil service of Sikkim was Chogyal's people. They could not be trusted beyond a point. I was a single man team from India to run the state. I was also deeply involved in political negotiations and most of the time went in meeting political leaders from all sides. The Chogyal never forgot to remind me that I was his appointee and could not go over his head. I had no access to intelligence directly that being an IB function under the Political Office.

After repeated requests by me to the Foreign Secretary, I was finally given three young IAS officers from West Bengal to assist me in running the administration. With their coming, I gave most of my time to political parleys. Finally, a breakthrough came in early May. The Political Officer, K.S. Bajpai, a professional diplomat, and I had to do some blunt speaking to the Chogyal reducing his choice to 'either' 'or'. Assuring him of his continued dynasty to rule as a constitutional head with some reserved powers to be exercised through the India-nominated Chief Executive, the Chogyal conceded the 'one man one vote' right. Fresh elections were to be held under a revised electoral roll.

After almost unbreaking and relentless negotiations, an agreement was finally signed on May 8, 1973, between the Foreign Secretary representing Delhi and the Chogyal. Neither side was fully satisfied but it paved the way for the ultimate turn of events, the merger of Sikkim with India.

An Election Commissioner, R.N. Sen, a very senior IAS officer, was given to me. While working with me as a Sikkim Government employee, he was under the overall umbrella of the Chief Election Commissioner of India. We went about a jet speed delimiting the electoral constituencies and finally the elections were held under the aegis of the Chief Election Commissioner. The anti-establishment party, Sikkim Congress, led by Kazi Lhendup Dorji, won 31 out of 32 seats. A new Government was installed. Second phase of my assignment was completed smoothly.

We had a smoothly running state in 1974 with me as head of the new administration. It was, however, not entirely smooth. The American wife of Chogyal, Hope Cooke and the Belgian wife of Kazi, were the new power centres. All had ambitions of their own, cutting at each other's throat. Sensing problems, the Executive Council was redesignated as Council of Ministers with the Kazi as Chief Minister. A new constitution was framed. Under this, there was a special provision of 'Association with Government of India'. The Chief Minister tabled a resolution on seeking close economic and political representation with India. All hell broke loose. The Chogyal was up in arms and so was the entire bureaucracy. The day this resolution was to be discussed in the Assembly, I was threatened personally for the first time. Telephone calls started coming in, supported by some intelligence that a grenade would be thrown in the Assembly premises to prevent the resolution from being taken up. I was presiding over the Assembly session that night. I walked into the Assembly all alone defying the threats and to reassure the members of Delhi's strength. The resolution was finally passed without any mishap.

Delhi accepted the Assembly's request for making Sikkim an Associate State providing Sikkim representation in the Indian Parliament. It was done under a constitutional amendment called the Thirty-sixth Amendment Act 1974.

I finally bade goodbye to Sikkim in September 1974, completing the task assigned to me. It was perhaps the most challenging task of my entire career. To correct a historical mistake, committed in 1948, was not easy. Sikkim was then a princely State with its ruler, the Maharaja, a member of the Chamber of Princes. The Sikkim Congress demanded merger with India in 1948. It was turned down by Delhi wanting to preserve the special relationship with the Himalayan Kingdoms of Nepal, Bhutan and Sikkim under the then prevailing treaties. That is how Sikkim's status as a protectorate of India was redefined under the Indo-Sikkim Treaty of 1950 retaining the historical role of the minority, the Bhutias, who ruled the State since the eighteenth century. With China occupying Tibet in 1950 and claiming Sikkim its territory and subsequent Sino-Indian war in 1962 made Sikkim extremely vulnerable to India's security.

The Chogyal wanted to acquire an independent sovereign country status for Sikkim and started his own campaign of India baiting. The Chinese intruded into Nathula, sensitive point on Tibet border. The Sino-Indian war convinced Delhi of the dangers. When the anti-Chogyal forces rose in 1973 to demand democratic rights and remove the Bhutia dominance, who constituted 11 per cent of the population, Delhi saw an opportunity to rectify a serious lapse committed in 1948. Foreign contacts plus Chinese claims on Sikkim led to the final count of the events of 1973-74.

The Associate State status decided in 1974 came under severe strain when the Chogyal began contacting China through Nepal. His American wife Hope Cook, who deserted him in 1974, was still active behind the scene. Other subversive elements also began to pose a possible threat. Trouble broke out again in 1975 between the Chogyal and the ruling party led by Kazi. Clashes occurred and the Sikkim Congress then demanded a referendum on removing the Chogyal and merger with India.

A referendum was held on these two issues. Overwhelming support was given and consequent to these results and on request of the Sikkim Assembly, the Government of India agreed to amend the Associate status to incorporation of Sikkim as a full fledged State of India under the Thirty-eighth Amendment Act of 1975. Thus, the Sikkim saga came to its conclusion.

10

A Police Failure – Its Fallouts and Lessons

P.S. RAMAMOHAN RAO

When one is called upon to reminisce on an experience in one's career, which made a profound impact on the course of events, the natural inclination would be to narrate a success story, which reveals one in good light and, perhaps, helps to boost the self image. John F. Kennedy said, "success has many fathers, but failure is an orphan". Though it may be hard to determine the paternity precisely, each participant in a successful endeavour would like to believe that he is the real source of such success. On the other hand, owning failure could lead to loss of face and self esteem.

In writing this memoir, I have deliberately chosen to write on failure, not because I need to prove the strength of my character nor on account of any suppressed need to relieve my conscience of a burden of guilt but in the sincere hope that it may help those, who read it, to draw conclusions, which may and can serve as lessons or guidelines for future action in similar circumstances.

In policing, post-mortems, with a view to future action, are hard to come by. Police move from situation to situation and from crisis to crisis, leaving them little time and even less inclination to pause and review each action in order to draw lessons for the future. Such 'post-facto' dissections of police action – as there are, largely relate to communal disturbances, done by Judicial Commissions, in which operational decisions of the police get submerged in political and legalistic assumptions and arguments. Seldom have we seen the report of any Judicial Commission providing a practical lesson to the police on handling of situations. In military operations, however, it is said, rather aptly, that when one war is over, the military starts training for the next by drawing heavily upon the lessons of the last one. This is possible since wars are not as frequent as law and order disturbances. Critical and detailed appraisals of each battle and war are undertaken and documented for the use of posterity. In this background, I hope that my narrative will serve a similar purpose.

The episode, I recount here, has in fact two parts. Though they are not organically connected to each other, yet they were so intertwined in time and from the operational point of view of the police that it becomes necessary to deal with both separately and, where necessary, together, in order to bring into perspective, the constraints and considerations, that shaped police responses and actions, which in effect, meant mine, as the Head of the police force of the state, when these events took place.

The year was 1988. Vijayawada, long considered the political hub of Andhra Pradesh, had, by then, been living for over 15 years with an endemic L & O problem of two rival mafias, constantly at each other's throat even while holding the city, which had been carved out into their respective spheres of influence, in perpetual awe and anxiety. Both sides ran parallel and informal, but effective systems of justice, in which disputes relating to land tenancy, money lending, marital relations and family disputes were being settled without reference or recourse to the official machinery of law. It all started towards the end of 60s, in the left wing student politics from which a militant student leader, who shall be known as 'R' for the purpose of this narrative, emerged. Over a period of time, he became such a threat to his parent organisation and also to certain sections of society that he was liquidated by his enemies. The leadership mantle of this mafia was then picked up by his younger brother, 'M'. In the meantime, a dissident faction, from within this mafia, emerged, under the leadership of Mr. 'G'. Soon the rival mafias became identified with two prominent castes of the area, to which the rival leaders belonged, on account of a number of local factors at work. Then Mr. 'G' was liquidated by the 'R' faction and the bitterness of the rivalry only grew. "G's" younger brother 'N' took over the leadership of this faction. Significantly, 'M' married a girl belonging to "N's" caste.

Both the groups, having drifted away from their initial left wing moorings, sought to get closer to the Congress Party, which ruled the State, without interruption, from the time of its formation in 1956. But the response from the Congress leadership was at best lukewarm till the Telugu Desam Party was founded by the Thespian, late NTR in dramatic circumstances in April-May, 1982. As the rivalry between the two mafias acquired a caste character, it wasn't difficult for Mr. 'N' to cosy up to N.T.R. and gain entry into his Party, as they belonged to the same caste. The popular image cultivated by 'N' of being some sort of a defender of the interests of his community had also helped. In the Assembly elections held in January 1983, which catapulted NTR into power, within eight months of his entering upon the political stage, 'N', who was adopted as the Telugu Desam candidate in one of the Vijayawada suburban constituencies, rode the NTR tide to become an MLA. A natural corollary to this was the admission of 'M' into the Congress Party soon after. In the mid-term Assembly elections, which took place in January 1985, in the wake of the dramatic removal of NTR from office and his equally dramatic come back, both 'M' and 'N' became M.L.As from two neighbouring constituencies of Vijayawada and the hostility became more intense in the conducive political climate. Belonging to the ruling party, 'N' enjoyed a psychological advantage over his rival.

I took over as the DG & IGP of the State on 31 March 1987, in what was interpreted by my detractors, as a choice of NTR, induced by the circumstance of my belonging to the same caste as his. In May 1987, 'N' struck to dispose of a close aide of 'M' in Vijayawada city. Within a year thereof, 'M' retaliated by getting 'DM', the younger brother of 'N', killed in an ambush on the highway, when 'DM' was returning from Nellore to

Vijayawada in a van. Therefore, the desire for revenge on the side of "N's" mafia was so intense and overwhelming that even the utmost police vigil was not sufficient guarantee against mutual reprisals.

In this background, policing in Vijayawada was beset with problems of acute political sensitivities and tight rope walking. Encouraged by the massive political mandate of NTR, the SP incharge of Vijayawada city, when NTR first assumed office in 1983, acted tough to bring the mafias under control. But his actions were seen as directed towards throttling 'M' more than 'N' and, in due course, dubbed as partisan. His replacement fared a little better but had to go owing to the displeasure of the ruling party for other reasons which, *prima facie*, had some merit. In the assessment that a woman might, on account of innate reserve and the consequent constraint on accessibility, be less vulnerable to accusations of partisanship, I posted a sober and generally well regarded woman IPS officer as SP. But soon, it was clear that she was not the answer to the city's problems. She was then replaced by an IPS officer who, though low in profile and mild of manner, acquitted himself well as the Deputy Commissioner of Police incharge of the communally sensitive area of the old city in Hyderabad.

Both the mafias had moles in the police hierarchy passing on information about police moves. Therefore, large scale transfers of police officers and ranks, out of Vijayawada city, identified with one or the other mafia, were also made only to invite the criticism, based on numbers, that the exercise was intended to tarnish the good name of policemen belonging to 'M's community. Since there was a greater proportion of policemen belonging to M's community in the lower ranks, this grievance *prima facie* appeared genuine. In fact, the replacements, for those moved out, by and large, belonged to the same communities.

Apart from these internal measures of an administrative nature, it had also been felt that instead of merely reacting to incidents of violence, preventive detention of the principal aides on either side, while leaving out the leaders, both of whom were M.L.As, could be undertaken to bring the mafias under control. But there was manifest reluctance on the part of the District Magistrate to authorise such detentions. A proposal in early 1988 was turned down. Beefed up with additional grounds and after proper legal vetting by those conversant with the law, the proposal was renewed around October, 1988, but the District Magistrate continued to demur, with a hint that a political nod from above would be necessary to act on the recommendation. When I took up the matter with the Chief Minister, the strategy found favour, but an appropriate signal to the District Magistrate was not forthcoming. This was the essence of the situation in Vijayawada in October-November, 1988.

After the murder of 'DM', younger brother of 'N', 'M' was on the defensive. Apart from frequently shifting base, often to places outside the state, he invoked the political support of the Congress by projecting, what was essentially a confrontation between two mafias, as a political fight between the Ruling Party and the Congress. The indulgence with which the Ruling Party treated 'N', in a way, lent credence and weight to his campaign. The Congress held a series of public meetings in the region, covering five districts, in the latter half of 1988, whipping up caste emotions of people belonging to "M's" caste. 'M' accompanied a Union Cabinet Minister to all these meetings, at which the main exhortation was that if any harm came to the life of 'M', those districts should go up in flames. The fears of 'M' were not unfounded as there was evidence of "N's" underlings stalking 'M' outside the State, with a view to his liquidation, if an opportunity came their way.

Around September, 1988, 'M', therefore, approached the police for providing security to his life. 'N' enjoyed that privilege from the time his brother was murdered. When the SP detailed two personal security officers for his protection, 'M' was not satisfied. He returned the two personal security officers, with his own prescription of the scale of security he needed. This was unacceptable to the police, as it was not only unreasonable but smacked of dictating terms. At this juncture, I should point out that, as the Police Chief, I had consistently taken the view that police protection to any one, including

M.L.As, in respect of whom, threat to life arose from their private activities and conduct and not from espousal of political or politico-social causes, would not be consistent with the rule of law. But the problem arose with reconciling my stand with the frequent occurrence of factional murders of persons who were also active in politics, for which the police received the flak in public. It became difficult to differentiate between what was political and what was personal. Provision of PSOs appeared the lesser of the two evils though, subsequently, this practice was so subverted that those enjoying such protection indulged in their trade with even greater freedom and impunity.

The next general election, due by January 1990, was already on the horizon. The anti-incumbency factor, against NTR and the Telugu Desam, was slowly gaining strength. The Congress was able to cause some damage to NTR's image through litigation in the High Court seeking a Commission of Enquiry into allegations of personal corruption. The judgment of the High Court lent substance to the allegations, though popular perception was different. Therefore, the Congress was slowly moving into a political overdrive against the Ruling Party with its sight firmly set on the next general elections to the Lok Sabha and Legislative Assembly. The public meetings in the coastal districts in support of 'M' were part of this offensive.

The Congress Party opened another front in the form of an agitation in Rayalaseema districts alleging neglect of the region with regard to irrigation facilities and seeking a greater share of Krishna water. The agitation was to reach its apogee in a demonstration before the State Secretariat on 1 November, A.P. Formation Day, which would end with the submission of a memorandum to the Chief Minister. Hard intelligence pointed to the danger of the demonstration turning into a 'gherao' of the Secretariat and an invasion of the demonstrators into the Secretariat premises, by using the excuse of presentation of memorandum to the CM as "the thin end of the wedge". The plan was pregnant with the danger of serious violence, which could be exploited to great political advantage. To the police, the violence in the Secretariat compound including unprecedented vandalism in the CM's chambers, indulged in by Government employees in late 1986, was still fresh in memory. Therefore, as a counter strategy, it was decided that the Chief Minister should not attend office and instead receive the memorandum at the gate itself, after the ceremonial functions of the 'Day' were over. It was also agreed that the assembly of demonstrators should be kept away at a safe distance from the Secretariat in order to minimise the possibility of their storming into the Secretariat. Avoidance of the use of force at all costs was the essence of the police strategy.

As the ceremonial pageant was going on, dividing the attention of the city police, the demonstrators managed to congregate in front of the Secretariat main gates and the plan of keeping them at a safe distance had to be abandoned. By the time the celebrations were over and the CM reached the Secretariat gates, the assembly was over 5000 strong with more volunteers trickling in. The Congress Party leadership was present in full strength with Union Cabinet Ministers in the front. The offer of the Chief Minister to receive the memorandum at the main gate was, predictably, turned down and instead an audience in the chambers of the CM was insisted upon. The inevitable confrontation started. Thereupon, the Chief Minister, used his histrionic experience to take everybody by surprise and shift the spotlight from the demonstration to himself by squatting on the middle of the broad road in a 'counter dharna'. As his partymen also mustered in strength, he went one step further to lie down in the middle of the road. The CM's 'coup' went beyond what was broadly agreed upon in the strategy discussion held earlier. The Congress Party was totally caught unawares. Any initiative towards violence from the demonstrators would be counter-productive. On the other hand, provoking the police into use of force would be an ideal response which would subserve their political purposes. The best way to achieve this was obviously to target the police.

Thus oral taunts, paper balls, chappals and such other missiles, which would not hurt the police, but could still provoke them into action, started raining at frequent intervals. These were complemented and supplemented with exhortations by party leaders through microphone installed by them, at the venue. Our instructions to the police were to act only if the demonstrators resorted to violence and otherwise to resist all provocations with patience and stoicism. At times, the provocation was so grave that it became a herculean task to restrain the police rank and file. Apart from other field police officers, the Commissioner of Police and I were on our feet, without sitting even for a few minutes, for over six hours to hold the police force in check and ensure that they bore all insults and provocations in good humour. It was one of the greatest tests of patience and sense of humour that I was a witness and party to. The confrontation ended, at about 5.30 PM, as dramatically as it started. The CM suddenly got up, walked to the place where the Congress Party leaders had assembled, snatched the memorandum from one of them and left the place in his car leaving the entire crowd stunned and stranded. With their patience worn out, they were in no mood to persist with the demonstration in any way. Disappointed and dejected and crestfallen, they slowly melted away to announce, the next day, that the agitation would be continued with a 'siege' of the Collectorate in Anantapur in Rayalaseema on 21-22 December, 1988.

Events in Vijayawada had, in the meantime, upstaged the proposed 'siege' at Anantapur. In the middle of December, 1988, police intercepted a van carrying the followers of 'M' to a nearby village for settling a local dispute. The van contained sticks and spears which could be lethal. Promptly, as if waiting for an opportunity, 'M' embarked upon a 'fast unto death' alleging that there was no security to the 'life and limb' of himself and his followers under the Telugu Desam Government. He would not explain how an expedition with a van, carrying lethal weapons, besides his followers, was a measure of protection to his own life. The venue of the 'fast' was on the pavement of a highway in front of his house, obviously calculated to attract and mobilise public attention and sympathy.

On receipt of the news about the 'fast unto death' from SP, Vijayawada, I briefed the Chief Minister and presented my appreciation of the situation on the following lines. The 'fast' presented a great opportunity for cutting down 'M' to size if only there was a reasonable assurance that no harm would be done to him from "N's" side. If "N's" goons stayed away from 'M', then the police could maintain peace and allow 'M' to stay on his fast, till an appropriate time when he would be arrested and shifted to a hospital. This would help the police to repudiate his contention by pointing out that if no harm came to him while he was lying in a public place for 10 days or more, he couldn't really complain of lack of safety. The strategy implied that, if the ruling party could restrain and discipline 'N', who was their MLA, the police would take care of 'M'. It would enable the police to put down the unlawful activities of the mafias in Vijayawada, even while satisfying the ruling party that their man was not being equated with his enemy. The CM seemed to appreciate and endorse the course of action outlined by me. This assessment was also shared with the Home Minister.

Accordingly, the SP, Vijayawada, was asked to hold his hand till the Congress 'siege' of Anantapur Collectorate was over, when police forces in sufficient strength could be moved to Vijayawada and 'M' could be picked up for "attempted suicide". It is appropriate to point out here that during this period, the A.P. police were even normally overstretched with most of the strength of the Armed Police deployed in the 'naxalite' infested districts and the Centre, not forthcoming with CRPF help in the measure, the situation warranted, for reasons, which seemed as political, as of resource constraint. Therefore, it was assessed that with the remaining manpower, it could be risky to open two fronts at the same time – one in Anantapur and the other in Vijayawada. The cardinal mistake in this strategy, as it turned out later, was to let the guard down on 'N', hoping that the ruling party and the CM would hold him on the leash. This did not, however, happen.

Thanks to some tactful handling by the District Magistrate, Anantapur, the Congress 'siege' of Anantapur Collectorate passed off peacefully on 22 December. The police forces, deployed there in some strength, were available for movement to Vijayawada, where tension was building up both on account of the desperation of the Congress at the 'fast' not being given the expected importance by the Government and the apprehension of "N's" community that "M's" supporters would unleash violence targeted at them. Nevertheless, the situation appeared under control and capable of being managed till the passing of Christmas when the arrest of 'M' could be carried out in accordance with the plan already discussed with the Chief Minister.

The decision to put off the arrest of 'M' till after Christmas would bear a little explanation. In the lower ranks of the police, there is a high proportion of Christians, most of them *dalit* converts. The A.P. Armed Police was one of the most over worked arms of the Government at that time, with the men separated from their families for extended periods and the nature of their deployment, most often, denying them even basic comforts. It was, therefore, considered both humane and necessary for morale to give them a break for Christmas and move them to Vijayawada on 26 December, when the decision to arrest 'M' could be implemented. Instructions went accordingly to all concerned.

In a total undoing of this plan, 'N' struck in the small hours of the night of 25/26 December, between 3 and 3.20 a.m. Nearly a dozen of his aides, led by his cousin 'D.R.', raided the venue of the 'fast', with axes and similar lethal weapons, and attacked 'M', who was sleeping, surrounded by more than a dozen of his trusted followers. Fatal blows were dealt on 'M'. In the melee, two others were also grievously injured, one of them by a bullet. In less than 10 minutes, the operation was over and the assailants, who came in a bus, vanished from the scene. [('D.R.' became MLA in 1994 when NTR returned to power and became a minister in 1997. He met with a gory death in a major railway accident in 1998).] 'N', himself, remained at home, and, when the news was broken to him, fled the city, accompanied by his police gunman. The timing and precision, with which the operation was conducted, gave room to a strong suspicion that "N's" mafia had an inkling that the police were likely to arrest 'M' immediately after Christmas and they would miss the best opportunity to eliminate 'M' if they delayed the matter. Later, investigations revealed that a couple of dummy runs of the operation preceded the actual attack. On the other hand, this daring operation led to the inference that no advice of restraint, much less caution, was received by 'N' from his party or the CM.

'M' was rushed to the Government General Hospital, close by, and was pronounced dead. As the news of the death spread, hell broke loose in Vijayawada city, with the caste supporters and sympathisers of 'M', who mostly consisted of lumpen elements, coming out into the streets and indulging in arson and loot of establishments and houses belonging to "N's" community. There was clear evidence of prior planning in the violence. Fire tenders were first immobilised by deflating tyres. Police stations were put under 'siege' by attacking them, with sufficient numbers of agitators, at each place. Repeated attacks were mounted on targets, identified with the ruling party. Most of the damage took the form of arson and loot. While arson was directed at business establishments, looting took place in residential neighbourhoods, where criminal elements, belonging to the community of 'M', and even others, took advantage of the situation and openly broke into houses of neighbours belonging to the community of 'N' to help themselves with whatever they could The situation could be brought under reasonable control only by about the mid-afternoon, whereafter there were only sporadic and minor incidents. Police action left 19 dead in police firings. The first firing took place at about 5 a.m. in front of the Government General Hospital, when the agitators went berserk.

The only death in the violence was of a medical doctor, who was identified with the Ruling Party, and took more than usual interest in prevailing upon the police to act against some lumpen followers of 'M', in his neighbourhood, who became a social menace. The occasion was used to settle scores against him and his defiant stance in bringing out a gun to confront his assailants sealed his fate. The doctor was a close friend of mine and only minutes before he was attacked, I had telephoned him from Hyderabad to get an independent assessment of the situation. I had offered to arrange protection for him and his family, which he did not feel necessary.

Nevertheless, I had cautioned him to be careful, keeping in view the nature of the conflagration that engulfed the city, and his own vulnerability.

The SP, Vijayawada, woke me up at 3.45 a.m. on the fateful morning to convey the bad news. I told him to hold firm and use firing as his first option at the earliest sign of violence, till I was able to rush enough police reinforcements to the City to take control. I then rang up the Home Minister and within 15 minutes thereof, we were both on our way to the CM, who was camping in his Film Studio, on the outskirts of the city. Well before 5 a.m., we met him and broke the ominous tidings. There was clearly a pause before he reacted to the news and endorsed my view that I should be left free to handle the situation. He had agreed that I should at once get on to the job. Within 10 minutes the HM and I left the CM and reached the Police Headquarters by about 5.30 a.m. to set up an operations' Control Room. My first task was to alert Superintendents of Police of all the neighbouring districts to move into a crisis mode and take all the precautions and operational measures to deal with any outbreak of violence. While S.Ps. of West Godavari and Krishna were readily available, their counterparts in Guntur, East Godavari and Nalgonda were away on tour and took time to establish contact.

My next step was to mobilise forces from wherever they were available, both within and outside the state, as I had anticipated a major and prolonged law and order situation in the state. Apart from instructions to the Armed Police Battalions at Mangalagiri, which is only 12 kms. from Vijayawada, Kurnool and Kakinada, I had also to tap the Hyderabad City Police and the Hyderabad Battalions to mobilise sufficient strength for deployment in Vijayawada and the neighbouring districts in accordance with the need. Thereafter, I got in touch with the Police Chiefs of Maharashtra, Madhya Pradesh, Orissa, Tamil Nadu and Karnataka to seek their help. My long tenure with the Central Government and my personal equation with all of them greatly facilitated their ready willingness to help (except Karnataka), unmindful of the political configurations in these states.

Simultaneously, I directed my attention to the needs of operational command. Obviously, the situation demanded upgrading of the command and deployment of a number of officers at the level of SP to take charge of the affected areas for concentrated attention and quick responses. This was where luck played truant completely. The I.G. (Law & Order) celebrated the marriage of his son on the Christmas day and was hosting a reception on the fateful day. I thought that it would be correct to move him to Vijayawada only after the reception was over. The I.G. (Intelligence) availed of the Christmas holiday to go out of town and was expected back at work only later in the morning. The I.G. (CID) was on his way to Tirupati and could be contacted only minutes before he was to board the plane at the Hyderabad airport, and asked to cancel his trip and proceed to Vijayawada to take charge of the situation. The I.G. (Administration) was the only senior officer readily available and he took charge of the operations' Control Room, as I was engaged in the tasks of mobilising and regrouping the forces to deal with the situation. DIG of Police, Eluru Range, who controlled Vijayawada city, was in hospital, having broken a leg in a motor accident. The DIG, Guntur was holding additional charge. To my consternation, he was still in Guntur at about 7.30 a.m., though the place was only 30 kms. away from Vijayawada. I contacted him last, having taken it for granted that he would have moved to Vijayawada as soon as the news reached him. But it was not the case and I had to literally chase him out of Guntur. Later, it transpired that he was actually in Vijayawada at the Railway Station to see off some relatives going back to Bihar, when the murder occurred. Having got the news, he chose to go back to his Headquarters by making a hair splitting distinction between informal tidings and official intimation. I also alerted a number of officers in Hyderabad city to move to Vijayawada as quickly as possible to assist the IGP (CID). To our ill-luck, the state helicopter was not available, having been grounded for periodic servicing. A hotline between the operations' room and the SP's office in Vijayawada was set up with the help of Telephone Department. By the time all these operational and logistic arrangements could be made, it was about 9.00 a.m.

As soon as the news of "M's" murder spread across the State, the Congress Party entered the fray alongwith the supporters of 'M' from his community. There were reliable reports pointing to exhortations from Congress Party office and leaders, to their local units and activists, to stir and stoke up trouble. Within hours, there were road blocks on the highways leading to Vijayawada, besides arson in a number of towns in the four districts of Krishna, Guntur, West Godavari and East Godavari. Stray demonstrations and violence were also reported from Prakasam and Nalgonda districts.

In particular, Guntur, the Headquarters of the district by the same name, Machilipatnam, district Headquarters and Gudivada in Krishna district, and Bhimavaram (West Godavari Distt.) bore the brunt of violence, clearly targeted at persons identified with the ruling party, irrespective of whether they were in politics, business or in professions. Some of the interior areas of Krishna district, where the caste rivalry between the two communities was longstanding and fairly intense, the community of 'N' was subjected to a few shameful atrocities.

The nature and pattern of violence left little doubt that the warnings repeatedly uttered at Congress sponsored public meetings in the region prior to the incident were being fulfilled and the Congress Party was more than keen to exploit the situation. The road blocks, erected in districts like Nalgonda, Khammam, Kurnool and Prakasam, in which the presence of the community to which the deceased 'M' belonged, was nominal, clearly betrayed the involvement of Congress activists.

As a result of such road blocks, the various police contingents mobilised from outside Vijayawada, as also the team of IPS officers despatched from Hyderabad, under the leadership of the IGP (CID), took inordinately long time to reach Vijayawada. They had to resort to many detours to reach their destination. To cite only one telling example, the reinforcements from Mangalagiri Armed Police Battalion, which was only12 kms. away, took nearly 1½ hours to reach Vijayawada. The DIG, Guntur, fared no better. Thus till 10 AM, the SP Vijayawada had to manage the situation on his own without much help. Another major handicap he had to cope with was the skeleton strengths available in all his Police Stations. As per time honoured practice, most of the night duty personnel in the Police Stations had left for their homes at around 3 AM. The day duty police personnel were to report for duty only at 7 AM. The occurrence of the 'murder' in the interregnum and the rapid eruption and spread of violence immediately thereafter prevented the day duty policemen, most of whom stayed in private accommodation widely dispersed in the city, to muster the courage of venturing out in police uniform to report for duty. Consequently, the Police Stations had only skeleton strength. Protection of Police Stations from marauding attackers became their primary and sole concern, leaving them no strength or scope to go to the help of business establishments and others, who became targets of violence and arson. As the SP declared curfew in the city, through the local Radio Station, in compliance with my instructions, shop keepers and businessmen did not venture out and this further facilitated the vandalism of the agitators. The imposition of curfew came in for heavy criticism which, in hindsight, seemed valid. The argument was that, if the owners of shops and business establishments had been allowed to defend themselves, instead of relying on police, they could have avoided a lot of destruction through arson as also looting. Of course, it is a moot point, if they would have dared to leave their homes and go to their places of business in the atmosphere of anger and violence that seized the city immediately after the murder.

Thus, till about 9.30 a.m., the city was largely at the mercy of the law breakers. Even in the midst of my preoccupation with the task of marshalling and deploying forces and officers to handle the extraordinary situation, I was in regular touch with the SP to build up his morale and exhort him that firing should be the only police response to violence, wherever possible. From about 10 a.m., the police, strengthened by reinforcements from outside, slowly regained the initiative and confidence. By about 2 p.m., violence came down to sporadic incidents and the city was left with a death toll of 19 in police firings and a sole victim at the hands of the agitators. In and around the neighbouring Guntur town, there were eight more deaths in police firings. By the time the IGP (CID) and other officers reached Vijayawada by about 3.30 p.m., the situation was eerily quiet, though tense. The IGP (L&O) and more reinforcements moved to Vijayawada by the next morning (27 December).

There was little doubt that the Congress Party would exploit the murder to its maximum advantage. Congress leaders, including Union Cabinet Ministers from the State, descended on Vijayawada in full strength. The dead body was moved to a maidan, not merely to enable mourners to go round, but to rouse the followers into more violence, if possible. The funeral date was delayed and word was spread that the Union Home Minister would visit the city to pay his homage to the 'slain leader' as a prelude to imposition of President's Rule. When the IGP (L&O) went to discuss the funeral arrangements, the Union Cabinet Minister, who had been the force behind 'M', in the months prior to the murder, treated him with scant courtesy and barely concealed contempt. Open demands were made even by responsible leaders for my suspension and dismissal from service. The air was thick with the expectation that President's Rule was indeed only days away. In fact, the overall situation was fraught with greater threats to law and order than had been confronted on the day of murder. How to maintain peace till the funeral and ensure that the funeral itself would pass off without any major incidents became problems of grave concern to the police.

Owing to some quiet lobbying conducted by me through the bureaucratic network, the idea of the Home Minister visiting Vijayawada was dropped. As regards President's Rule, obviously wiser counsels prevailed in Delhi, though to the great disappointment of the Union Cabinet Minister, whose hostility to the Chief Minister had always tended to be personal and openly insulting and whose conduct during those difficult days, fell far short of the standards of dignity and decorum expected of such highly placed and responsible persons. Through a process of intense and prolonged consultations between me and my principal staff officers, particularly the IGP (L&O), who was on the spot, a three pronged strategy was decided upon. It was agreed that the turnout at the funeral should be restricted to manageable limits even while saturating Vijayawada city with police presence. Concomitantly, all the main highways leading to Vijayawada should be adequately patrolled to control the infiltration into Vijayawada for attendance at the funeral. Similarly, the police presence and movement in all towns, within a distance of 100-150 kms., should be sufficiently intensified to deter "M's" sympathisers from any contemplation to proceed to Vijayawada to attend the funeral. To my great relief, the strategy was ably implemented by the various police officers entrusted with the responsibility and the funeral passed off with just a few minor incidents on the highways. Police conducted themselves with great restraint and responsibility in the face of insults and acts of provocation.

On 29-31 December, I accompanied the Chief Minister on a tour to all the towns, which had been rocked by major incidents of violence. We visited Machilipatnam, Gudivada, Bheemavaram, Guntur and Vijayawada. The CM was treated to harrowing tales of violence perpetrated by agitators belonging to "M's" community and also of police 'ineptness' in handling the situation. Considering that these narratives came from the victims, most of whom were ardent supporters of the CM, there was some element of exaggeration, but it was clear that at most places, police response and action were marked by diffidence. Where the police officers belonged to the community of 'N', the diffidence was palpable. But it struck me that, more than anything else, the strong political overtones of the murder inhibited normal responses from field police officers, all of whom belonged to the State. If those belonging to "N's" caste felt inhibited on account of the murder perpetrated by their own caste men, others belonging to the victim's caste were not inclined to be firm against their own caste men reacting in violence.

I stayed behind in Vijayawada on 31 December, 1988 to 1 January, 1989 to review the situation and lay down the guidelines for the future, particularly in regard to investigation of the various cases arising from the aftermath of the murder. Nearly, 20 teams of CID were constituted to go round all the affected places to collect complaints and register cases which numbered more than 1500. A special team under a Superintendent of Police, CID, who did not belong to the area, was formed to investigate the murder itself. As regards the wider issues surrounding the murder and the manner of its handling by the police, the Chief Minister had already announced the appointment of a Judicial Commission at the level of a High Court Judge. I held a press conference on 1 January to convey these various operational measures undertaken by the police to collect the pieces and restore normalcy. Though, at the very outset, I made it clear that the meeting should be confined to factual matters and all matters of judgment should be left to the Judicial Commission, I was still asked whether I saw a conspiracy in the pattern of violence. I replied I could not say if there was a conspiracy or not, placing it in the context of my introductory remark that all posers of a judgmental nature should be left to the Judicial Commission. I returned to Hyderabad on 2 January, 1989.

My straight faced response, that I could not say if there was a conspiracy or not, was twisted by the press, which carried on front pages the next day their coverage of my press conference to state that I had ruled out a conspiracy behind the violence. It appeared as if all the press reporters, who attended the press meet, collectively decided on this 'take' of my remark. There was a commotion in the Ruling Party and I was being bombarded with telephone calls as to the veracity of the press version, forcing me to issue a clarification which, true to form, did not get the same prominence in the next day's papers.

In those early hours of 26 December, when the Home Minister and I were proceeding from the Chief Minister's film studio to my office, we discussed the possible political fallout of the murder. The HM indicated that he would like to resign at the appropriate time owning moral responsibility for the murder. Accordingly, on 31 December, the Home Minister submitted his resignation from the Cabinet.

When the news of the death of my doctor friend at the hands of the agitators reached me in the morning of 26 December, I had also decided to quit as the Police Chief as soon as things were brought under control. Vijayawada is my home town, where I was born and educated till the age of 16years, when I left the place for higher studies. Apart from the loss of the life of a good friend, a large number of well wishers of mine and our family had suffered in various forms in the violent aftermath of the murder. On deep introspection, after the initial emotional impulse, I had come to the conclusion that, while I had nothing to be ashamed of in regard to the manner in which the post-murder situation was handled and brought under control, the murder itself was the outcome of the failure of my strategy on handling the hunger strike of the deceased. Having chosen a line of action, and discussed it broadly with the Chief Minister, I became complacent and did not cover my flanks by ensuring that proper tabs were kept on the intentions and moves of 'N' and his lieutenants. I took it for granted that 'N' would make no moves to settle his scores with 'M'. That, in my view, was a grave miscalculation. There was a clear failure of intelligence on the intentions and activities of 'N'. As for the handling of the violent aftermath, my professional judgment was that after the initial nervousness and inadequacy of response on the part of the local police leadership, we had done reasonably well to bring the situation under control as quickly as possible and even better in checkmating the designs to foster and prolong the climate of violence in the region.

In my long innings with the I.B. and after my return to the state police, I was involved, directly or indirectly, in about half a dozen major disturbances of law and order, arising from communal and political causes, most of which were protracted to extend over long periods of time. I had not known a single instance in any of them when, in a single day, as many as 27 persons were killed in police firings. I have no doubt in my mind that, but for effective police action, the situation could not have been brought under control in a single day, though the popular perception was that the police response was timid and tardy.

Nevertheless, I realised that my leadership would come under attack by my detractors. I sincerely believed, based on my career graph, that my appointment, as the Police Chief on

31 March 1987, bypassing the claims and aspirations of four of my seniors, was a recognition of my track record and not the result of extraneous considerations of caste or community. Till then all my rank promotions, except the ones I had earned during the NTR's regime, were accelerated and came ahead of what had been the norm. Apart from my all India rank in the initial competitive examination and the post-training tests, I was one of the five from my batch selected from all over India through a rigorous screening process for long term deputation to the I.B. where, by all accounts, I had done well. My stewardship of the APSRTC, before I became the DGP, for a record tenure of nearly 5½ years, earned widespread acclaim and many awards, both for the Corporation and myself. In fact, when I was chosen to be the Police Chief, I was not the first preference of the CM, but I was the choice of an overwhelming majority of the people including my predecessor, whom the CM had consulted before the appointment. The CM had himself confided in me to this effect. In this background, the popular Telugu saying that 'one should not sell fuelwood where he once sold flowers' kept on bothering my mind. It was a moment of truth and a test of the value system I believed in.

For all these reasons, I came to the considered conclusion that I should not continue as the head of the State Police. Accordingly, on the morning of 3rd January before the clarification to the press was issued, I sent a letter to the Chief Minister, owning responsibility for the happenings of the week and seeking my relief from the post of DG & IGP, A.P. I stated as follows in the letter:

> "In respect of officers placed in high positions and entrusted with critical responsibilities, the principle of job security cannot extend to condoning results, which are adverse to the interest and image of the Government. In this background, I can't be true to my conscience and the good traditions of civil service if I continue to remain at the helm of affairs in the Police Department".

When the press met the CM later in the afternoon to ascertain his reaction to my press remarks at Vijayawada on the previous day, he took the sting out of the ploy by revealing the substance of my letter. He did not, however, indicate his response to my request. But he made it known to his close advisors that he was not inclined to act on it. His subsequent dealings with me were also reflective of this mood.

But things slowly began to change. This was because I tried to run the Police Department as a taut and tight ship, giving no quarter to indiscipline, slackness of performance, particularly in the senior IPS ranks, and political interference in pursuance of partisan vested interests as opposed to the public good. Also, in the confidence of the full backing from the Chief Minister, I had pursued a vigorous and uncompromising campaign against corruption at all levels in the police. Obviously, such a pro-active and assertive style of leadership did not go well with those affected by such an approach, particularly senior IPS officers, who couldn't indulge in their accustomed ways of dalliance. They started to slowly work on the theory that, in failing to prevent the murder of 'M' and the outbreak of violence in Vijayawada and the surrounding areas thereafter, I did not live up to the confidence and expectations, which lay behind my choice as the Chief of Police, in preference to the claims of my seniors. The internal power struggle and equations in the Ruling party had also lent strength to this whispering campaign. My fears of my detractors mounting a campaign, though behind the scenes, were slowly coming true. Despite the respect and regard the CM continued to show towards me, he openly harboured the feeling that I did not act, as per his wishes, to change the SP at Vijayawada, a fortnight before the murder. He was convinced that the new SP would have been able to handle the violence more competently. The argument was not that the new SP would have prevented the murder, but would have handled the post-murder situation better. Obviously, there was a discord between the CM's appreciation and my own in this regard.

Therefore, I felt that I should press for my relief and should, under no circumstances, stay beyond the budget session of the Legislative Assembly, which normally commenced in early February and concluded at the end of March. Understanding my feelings in the matter, the CM slowly veered round to my stand, of course egged on by those, both within the party and outside, who were not favourably disposed towards me. Some disturbing developments in the first week of February helped hasten his decision. A leak of a Cabinet paper on the forthcoming budget led to the advice to him that he should act firmly in the matter. For all his sangfroid, after the cataclysmic events at Vijayawada, the CM was inwardly concerned. As he was in the process of making up his mind, a very disturbing family development took place. The convergence of all these developments made him to act, as was his wont, in a dramatic manner. On 6 February, he sacked his entire Cabinet and also accepted my request to be relieved from the office of DG & IGP. We had a long meeting in the early hours of that day, after which he conveyed his decision to appoint me as Chairman, Hyderabad Allwyn.

Later in the day, he clarified to the Chief Secretary, when he took the formal proposal to appoint me as Chairman and Managing Director, that for one, who had served as the Police Chief, it would be honourable and appropriate to function only as Chairman and not look after the day to day running of the company also. Till my retirement, I was the only bureaucrat who was retained as a Chairman of a Public Sector enterprise. All other Chairmen were politicians, who could not be accommodated in the Cabinet. Other bureaucrats, who were senior to me, served only as Vice Chairmen and Managing Directors. This was a clear message to me that, though I had lost his confidence, I did not lose his respect. Of course, within six months thereafter, when the murder of a Panchayat Mandal Parishad President by the naxalites rattled the Government, the CM sent for me and requested that I should go back to the Government as his advisor on law and order and security. I politely declined the suggestion on the ground that I would not like to become a rival centre of power and authority to the DG & IGP and thereby detract the status and stature of an office, which I had myself held before.

In November, 1989, general elections to the Lok Sabha became due. "NTR" advanced the general elections to the Legislative Assembly, normally due in January, 1990, to synchronise with the Lok Sabha polls, in the calculation that it would work to the advantage of his Party. But after having campaigned for the opposition throughout the country and made a significant contribution to the defeat of the Congress, he was voted out of power in his own state. His party fared poorly in the Lok Sabha polls also. Congress returned to power after 7 years, only to resume its old ways of governance. As in the previous tenure, the office of the Chief Minister changed hands thrice and internal squabbles were waged and carried to the extent of mutual denigration and damage. The community of 'M', which shifted its loyalty to Congress wholesale, became disillusioned and influential sections thereof drifted back to Telugu Desam by the time of the next Assembly elections in November 1994. Prohibition and continuance of the Rs. 12 per kg. rice scheme became bones of contention between the Congress and Telugu Desam. Combining the public dissatisfaction on these issues with his own 'charisma', NTR rode back to power in November 1994 with a larger mandate than ever before. 'N' was made a minister. His cousin 'D.R.', who masterminded the murder of 'M', became an MLA. However, after NTR was eased out of office in August 1995, through an internal revolt in the party led by N. Chandra Babu Naidu, the present CM, 'N' became marginalised, but 'D.R.' became a minister, in one of the subsequent Cabinet reshuffles, only to lose his life in 1998 in a gory railway accident. 'N' promptly changed sides to join the Congress Party, while the wife of 'M', who became MLA in 1994 on Congress ticket, crossed over to the Telugu Desam. In the Assembly elections held in October 1999, 'N' was defeated by the Telugu Desam candidate. "M's" wife was not given a ticket by Telugu Desam Party. Both 'N' and "M's" wife remained active, but with their clout and influence greatly diminished. Other players have taken over the stage in Vijayawada, but are said to be lying low on account of the presence of a determined, effective, 'no nonsense' Commissioner of Police (Vijayawada city was converted into a Police Commissionerate sometime in 1990).

The case of murder of 'M' went through a tortuous process of investigation. After initial handling by the state CID, the case was transferred to the CBI on the insistence of the wife of the deceased 'M'. The case was charged against 40 persons including 'N', his cousin 'D.R.', and seven hired assassins. After 13 years, during which period much water flowed down the Krishna river, on whose bank Vijayawada is situated, the main dramatis personae switched political parties and witnesses were won over, the case was acquitted against all the accused in March, 2002.

I come to the end of this narrative of an intense struggle for supremacy between two mafias, which not only tested severely the style and substance of law enforcement, as also the instruments of policing, but had also a significant impact on the course of the political and social history of the Krishna-Godavari belt in Coastal Andhra Pradesh during the 90s. I have tried to be as candid as possible in tracing the events. In addition, I have made a sincere effort to be objective in narrating facts and presenting the popular construction of the various events. What could be the lessons for the police from this episode ?

In the many aspects, in which policing differs from the defence of the frontiers, the most prominent one is the use of force. In a war, no holds are barred and supremacy of fire power on land, in the air and on the seas is the key to the outcome. But in maintenance of law and order and internal peace, use of firearms is the last option and a measure of the last resort. Even so, in situations, where raw animal instincts of human beings tend to overwhelm the rules of normal and civilised human behaviour, early and effective use of firearms becomes necessary for the police even in maintenance of order. The experience in Vijayawada amply demonstrated the validity of this approach.

However, the best policing consists in prevention of threats to peace and order, rather than effective control and putting down of violence after peace is broken. Timely and adequate intelligence is a *sine qua non* to good policing. The catastrophic disturbances in Vijayawada and the surroundings were the result of failure of intelligence regarding the moves and machinations of "N" and his cohorts. But within police forces, the importance of intelligence, particularly at the ground level, tends to be 'sadly' discounted. Boasts of being law and order types and disparaging remarks about intelligence personnel are common knowledge in police forces. This malaise has spread even to senior ranks manned by the IPS. Professional efficiency in police can be built up only on foundations of sound legal knowledge, sharp investigative skills and good intelligence craft and not by wielding the stick and shooting from the hip. In the instant case, good intelligence would have helped the police in preventing the murder of 'M' and the disastrous consequences thereof.

Preventive policing is heavily dependent on the timely and effective use of the powers of detention. If only the District Magistrate in Vijayawada had shared the appreciation and concern of the local police with regard to the need to immobilise the rival mafias, he would not have rejected or sat upon the proposals of the SP for preventive detention of the leading lights of either group other than the leaders themselves. With the increasing orientation of Collectors towards development administration, the time has come to seriously debate the merits of investing senior police officers with magisterial powers of preventive detention uniformly instead of limiting them to Commissionerate of Police.

Apart from lack of intelligence, complacence could be a self defeating delinquency for police. In fact, policing in any situation should be based on the 'worst case scenario' in order to be prepared for all contingencies. Vijayawada was a telling example of how a complacent assumption on my part that 'N' would do no harm to 'M' spelt disaster.

Policing in India is a complex task unlike in Western democracies. It is not a linear transaction that can be conducted in black and white. The extreme stratification of Indian society, both vertically and horizontally, on account of the bewildering diversities of race, religion, region, community, caste, culture, social and economic developments renders policing, most of the time, a balancing act among show of authority, application of law, use of force, counselling under the cloak of authority, timing of actions and political rivalries. For these reasons, the

Western model of placing the police under the local authorities is unlikely to work and may even prove dangerous. Given the fractionalism and the resultant factionalism in Indian society, the placement of police under local authority will make them the storm troopers of the party or faction or caste in power. It was in appreciation of this reality that the British created an elitist command in the form of Indian Police subject, further, to the general control of the Indian Civil Service. The same reality prompted Sardar Vallabhbhai Patel to continue this legacy in the shape of the Indian Police Service and Indian Administrative Service. The Vijayawada episode will illustrate all the elements of the tight rope walking that police are faced with in confronting and dealing with threats to law and order, which have overtones of caste, culture, social attitudes and political affiliations.

I have deliberately omitted corruption from this analysis. If one factors in this evil also, the problems of policing and effective command and control over the police ranks become even more intractable.

The political control of the ruling party over the police is widely held as responsible for ineffective and distorted policing which, therefore, affords little relief to those affected by crime and violations of law and order. The National Police Commission examined this malady and recommended (a) constitution of State Security Commission to oversee the police, (b) selection of the Police Chief by the said Commission, and (c) a fixed tenure for the Police Chief so appointed. It is no surprise that the political establishments in India have not bitten these proposals. No Chief Minister, irrespective of the political party, to which he belongs, would like to lose control of the police. But even setting aside this subjective consideration of political advantage, do these recommendations really provide the remedy? How will they work in practice ?

A Security Commission consisting of the Chief Minister/ Home Minister and the Leader of the Opposition will, in my view, only broaden the political pressures on the Police Chief and his vulnerability. The Commission itself can turn into a miniature Legislative Assembly. In a country, where political discourse finds it impossible to accommodate bipartisan view on even national issues, one has to be sceptical of the efficacy and practicality of such arrangements as the Security Commissions.

I am not aware of any country where the Chief Executive is divested of the power and freedom of choice in key appointments. On the other hand, in the USA, such appointments made by the U.S. President, in his sole discretion, are subsequently subject to scrutiny by Senate Sub-Committees to ensure that the appointees are persons with impeccable credentials. It must be noted that such scrutiny does not extend to considerations of relative merits of candidates. Such a mechanism can be thought of even in India, provided it covers all crucial appointments.

A fixed tenure for the Police Chief, or for that matter any important post, is a good concept worthy of serious consideration. Even so, it is better to prescribe minimum and maximum tenures in order to provide flexibility in the event of a choice proving wrong or unsatisfactory. If the choice proves bad, a change can be effected after the minimum tenure. If it turns out good, the incumbent can continue upto the maximum tenure. Such a band of tenure will have the advantages of (a) providing for wider choice, (b) excluding candidates who have less service than even the minimum tenure, and (c) preserving the powers of the political executive to select the Police Chief and changing him at the end of the minimum tenure if he does not come up to expectations or turns out to be a bad choice.

Police is an instrument of law and can only be answerable to judiciary and not to oversight Commissions. However, complaints of malfeasance and misuse of power against police need to be carefully looked into, considering the powers and authority vested in them under law. Suitable institutional mechanisms have to be devised and established for this purpose instead of a supervisory Commission, having political character, as suggested by the National Police Commission.

I come now to one last but important issue, which has been of great interest and relevance to governance. How independent can the Police Chief or any one similarly placed, be of the political executive ? What should he do if there is a serious difference between him and the Chief Executive, or if the latter overrides the advice of the former? My experience and insights into the matter have convinced me that it will be wrong and impractical to expect and much less insist that the Police Chief should prevail every time there is a difference of opinion or assessment with the CM. It is axiomatic in management and leadership that what matters is the ultimate winning of a debate and not every point in the debate. Similarly in war, it is not necessary to win every battle. What matters is the ultimate victory in a war. Similarly, the Police Chief has to discriminate issues on the basis of their relationship to fundamental values and importance to outcomes. If there is no moral compromise involved, then the differences can only relate to perception or a view point and can't be the ground for confrontation. If a Police Chief were to consider exit every time there is a difference of opinion, there can be no administration or governance. During my tenure of nearly two years as Police Chief of A.P., I had frequent differences of opinion with the C.M. Here I must affirm that the C.M. had rarely interfered with my professional judgment or exerted political pressure except in cases where his partymen had complained of poor performance or serious delinquencies against individual police officers. But he would come up with ideas or proposals to reform the police which would amount to serious disruption or break with existing practices and conventions and can't be implemented in the given framework. His impatience with the pace of change or the implementation of a directive was another problem to contend with. There were occasions when I had seriously considered the option of leaving the post, but stayed due to persuasion by others close to the CM on the argument that continuance in command is more conducive not only to the implementation of the reform measures I had taken up but also to bringing about a transformation in the CM's understanding of the issues and problems involved. It was only when I felt that continuance any longer in the post would be fundamentally inconsistent with my value system that I chose to quit.

I remained undisturbed as Chairman, Hyderabad Allwyn, even after Congress returned to power. Congress leaders close to the new CM, with whom I had worked closely in his earlier tenure, began suggesting to me that I should go back as the Police Chief, but the suggestion did not come from the CM himself. Grapevine had it that those, who were closely aligned with 'M', were opposed to my heading the police force once again. The next Chief Minister was insistent that I should serve as the Home Secretary. After a great deal of persuasion from him, I reluctantly agreed to take up the assignment on certain conditions, which he had accepted. But formal orders of appointment never came. I had learnt later that those senior IPS officers, who had received adverse reports from me, when I was the Police Chief, lobbied hard against my appointment as Home Secretary. When I retired from the IPS on 31 July 1992, as the senior most IPS officer in the country, my tenure as Chairman, Hyderabad Allwyn, was extended, without my knowledge for six months, with the suggestion that I should remain in that office till the privatisation of the Company, which had been initiated by me, was complete. While I did not want to be discourteous to the Government by refusing the extension, I intimated to the Government that I would like to go at the end of the extension period or even before if the task were to be completed. Accordingly, I laid down the office of Chairman on 31 January 1993. During my tenure as Chairman, Hyderabad Allwyn, a number of offers to go to the Government of India came my way. While I did not consider many of them worthwhile to uproot myself from Hyderabad at that stage of my life, my proximity to NTR was held against me when my name was considered for one or two critical and prestigious assignments at the Centre.

11

Momentous Day in Service

D.C. NATH

If my failing memory suggests correctly, it should be some time in July, 1964. Young both at heart and spirit, I was then the Sub-Divisional Police Officer (SDPO) at the "prestigious" Serampore Sub-division of Hooghly district in West Bengal. The occasion was the *rathajatra* festival, the forward journey of Lord Jagannath by chariot, at Mahesh, a place perhaps second only to Puri in Orissa in terms of religious sanctity of this specific festival. The chariot of Lord Jagannath is on this occasion drawn for over a length of one or two furlongs on the historic Grand Trunk Road, which obviously remains closed to traffic for a prolonged period. On an average, about half a million people used to gather on the occasion – some to pull the chariot, some to put their hands on the rope drawing the chariot and a vast many to go round and enjoy the *mela* set up all around the place. The atmosphere could be as festive as one could imagine.

The police *bandobast* on the occasion was naturally elaborate. This young officer, bristling with energy and idealism, born of abundant love and affection bestowed on him by his seniors, felt literally thrilled and excited to be incharge of this pretty vast and all-purpose police arrangement. The duty of the policemen was not only to maintain law and order but also to facilitate smooth pulling of the chariot of Lord Jagannath by the members of the crowd assembled on the occasion. The saying goes that being able to touch the rope pulling the chariot washes away all the sins committed and so the frenzy to achieve that great religious feat of escaping the possible divine wrath due for misdemeanors and mischief in the mundane journey of human life.

The duty on the *rathajatra* day started since early morning. That was preceded by an elaborate briefing of the force gathered a couple of days before from different parts of the district. The morning did not show much of a promise to be a bright day. As a matter of fact, almost by regulation, it started raining early in the day. It is said some rain on this day of days is a must – a religious dictum so to say. But the showers gradually became very heavy and in no time all of us on duty got fully drenched from head to toe. In my case, it started with my newly-acquired peak-cap, going down to the starched-uniform and the well polished boots. To the credit of all officers and men on duty at their respective posts, I can proudly announce even today that not a single soul batted even an eyelid – no matter the inclement weather – and remained steadfast to their posts and duty. It was an experience for the SDPO to walk up and down the stretch of the chariot's route umpteen times in drenched uniform and continue to shout "shabash" to the men struggling to keep the crowd upbeat in their religious zeal in order. It would be worth mentioning that in view of the sensitivity and religious sanctity of the occasion, the policemen were totally unarmed, i.e., not even with sticks in their hands.

It so happened, the rain-god soon gave way to the sun-god and by mid-day, he was blazing and scorched us pretty well. It was then, as it was said, a "matter of luck" for those of us on duty that the crowd assembled on the day was one of the heaviest for the occasion. A modest estimate had put it to be above five lakhs. It was indeed tough-going to help people keep to any discipline in their thrust and urge to touch or pull the ropes of the chariot. The slushy underground – thanks to the earlier pouring rain – did not make things easy either. The journey of Lord Jagannath in the process got delayed, but eventually He reached the destination without much of fuss. But it was a "terrible" day for the policemen, if I may put it that way perhaps somewhat irreverently. The starched uniforms that had got drenched in the early hours of the day, got fully dried up by the afternoon even with the sweat and toil of the day and by the evening all of us looked like to be in sack-clothes but in khaki colour.

The day or the general duty got over by about 9.00 PM. After the crowd melted, a skeleton staff was posted for the night shift. By the grace of Lord Jagannath, the occasion passed off without any mentionable incident of undesirable activity or any breakdown in law and order situation. The sincere and hard work put in by the tireless and what appeared to me rather motivated men in uniform did not thus go in vain. The seniors gave us pat on the back and left some time later in the evening.

Feeling rather buoyed up by the success of the day, we then planned for a celebration-cum-debriefing session at the Mahesh outpost. The men and officers in their 'sack-clothes' assembled and after a round of sweets, the SDPO was to address the force. Finding it suitable to be a platform, I got up on top of an old oil barrel lying somewhere in the compound and lost no time in expressing my profound gratitude and thanks to the officers and men for their having indeed risen like a man and discharging their duty with most unswerving loyalty and devotion. I do not remember what all I had said but obviously I must have got carried away by the feeling of success and emotion swelling up in me. Almost immediately after I had finished my oration, reminding everybody to assemble again for similar duty after a week on the occasion of the *ultarath* and was about to jump off the oil barrel on which I was standing, some officers and men at the back spontaneously shouted, "SDPO "Sahab, Zindabad" SDP Sahab, Zindabad". The verve and the ring of sincerity in their shouting this appreciation even today ring in my ears as if all this had happened the other day. I must vouchsafe that was one of the proudest days in my not-so-distinguished career. The Lord has been kind to me and I have had some other almost similar occasions of having enjoyed the best of love and respect from junior colleagues, etched in memory. But the occasion briefly described here was the first such experience and hence the most momentous day in my service career. I take this opportunity once again to salute the bunch of dedicated people, the like of which it has been a privilege to work with. To my humble reckoning, it was not so much my leadership but my devotion to the officers and men on duty that had earned me the accolade, which, needless to add, I sincerely cherish, or rather shall cherish till the last breath. It was indeed a typical case of flowering of *esprit de corps*, a much needed requirement in a police force worth its salt.

12

Those Moments from the Yellow Pages

KALYAN K. MITRA

Wordsworth defined poetry as emotions recollected in tranquillity. But how does one define recollections of the past by a bureaucrat or policeman in the tranquil environ of the present ? The reminiscences of a public servant can never be poetical. In fact, quite the contrary. There is distinct danger of autobiographical notes degenerating into dull and boring accounts of the writer's achievements and moments of glory as he sees them. Let me, therefore, try and recount a few events of days long gone by, which are certainly not high points in my professional life. Rather, these were occasions which can be more appropriately described as learning experiences of a young impatient police officer.

In the sixties and the seventies, Orissa was an interesting place to be in, albeit, a little challenging for a city bred youngster like me who never learnt cycling and had no idea of how to light a hurricane lantern. In the small sub-divisional and district towns our only entertainment was listening to the radio or reading newspapers which used to come from Calcutta a day or two later. The local newspapers hardly carried the kind of news one gets to read in the metropolitan cities.

Then there was always the exciting prospect of going out on tours for inspection or supervision of cases. Driving mile after mile in the countryside was such a joy and the thrill of reaching a Dak Bungalow in a remote corner of the district is vividly recalled even today though so many years have passed.

And, of course, there were plenty of books and magazines to read. Hardly a week passed without at least one good book coming my way. The first thing I did wherever I went was to befriend the principal of the local school and college and use the library facilities. Besides, books were not all that expensive those days and we could order them by post. The advent of TV and the personal computer, though beneficial in many ways, has probably killed the simple pleasure of reading for many young entrants to service these days. I did not miss the glitz and glamour of big city life I was used to. Nor did I miss watching the latest English movies – a habit I formed during my student days in Calcutta.

There is much talk of corruption these days as there is all pervasive and ever- growing corruption in every branch of civil service, from the very top to the bottom. People were corrupt those days also. But corrupt senior officers were very few those days. The few, whose integrity was in doubt, were easily marked out and were shunned by colleagues in public as well as in social life. Most officers followed an unwritten code of conduct. We used to travel in our own cars and carry provisions, cooking oil, rice and even firewood while going out on tour from Headquarters, so that we did not have to depend on the resourcefulness of the police officer incharge or the Daroga Babu, who would given a chance, inevitably make the local grocery store owners look after the visiting boss. Of course, there were occasions when a sudden unplanned visit had to take place. On such occasions, the officer incharge of the Police Station or the outpost would, without fail, present a ridiculously deflated nominal bill for breakfast, lunch, dinner, etc. necessitating much negotiation and upward revision before the bill could be settled.

But sometimes we were carried away by our youthful arrogance and forgot that there were occasions when self-imposed rules needed to be violated. On a hot afternoon in the month of May, my wife and I were returning to our Headquarters in Puri by road. It was already 2 o'clock when we reached Khurda Police Station on the National Highway. We halted at the Police Station mainly for the driver of my car, who I thought needed a little rest and a meal. The officer incharge was, no doubt, quite surprised to see the Addl. SP and his wife but quickly made us comfortable in the inspection room. I ordered the constable, who was detained to look after us, to fetch tea and biscuits from a nearby tea shop. But sometimes later, we were offered a full meal and, being hungry, enjoyed the meal. Before leaving, I asked for the bill and was quite annoyed when the officer expressed his inability to accept any payment. When I insisted he replied that we were his guests and since his wife had prepared a rather simple meal herself, there was no question of presenting a bill. I had little choice but to accept his hospitality but did not conceal my annoyance for offering home cooked lunch without taking my permission. As I look back to the incident which took place almost forty years ago, I wonder why on earth I did not consider it necessary or appropriate to thank his wife personally or even write a letter to the officer later thanking him and his wife for kindness shown to us on that hot May afternoon ? Would it have diminished my authority if I had shown that gesture ? Or was it plain lack of consideration for a junior colleague? Later in life, I learnt that attention to little things in the life is important in human relationships. We tend to forget that people are sensitive inside and the ability to thank or apologise as and when necessary is not a sign of weakness. It is the weak who are insensitive to others.

In July, 1964, I was posted as the Superintendent of Railway Police with Headquarters in Cuttack, which also happened to be the Headquarters of the IG of Police, as the Police Chief was designated those days. I had state-wide jurisdiction and had a small saloon car at my disposal. I still recall the enormous joy of moving from one place to the other in that saloon car which, though small, had a large attached toilet with bath tub, pantry, a kitchen, a large cabin comfortable for two people and a saloon-orderly-cum-cook. We were also lucky to have been quickly allotted a nice bungalow with a garden behind the Stadium. Cuttack, being the biggest town of Orissa, seemed to be just the place for the two of us. There was also the good old Cuttack club within walking distance from our home. Life seemed to be well under control, but alas, like all good things, this period ended too soon.

In 1964, Orissa saw one of the worst communal killings in the history of the state which rocked the district of Sundargarh, the steel city of Rourkela and adjoining areas in Western part of the state. In village after village, innocent Muslims were killed by violent mobs of tribal youth, as false rumours spread that Government would reward any one who killed the Muslims. The initial spark that lit the communal fire was the tales of horror narrated by riot affected men, women and children displaced from the then East Pakistan who were being transported to refugee camps in trains which stopped *en route* at the Rourkela Railway Station. The entire administrative machinery was caught by surprise and the situation remained out of control for several days. The police administration came under severe criticism resulting in a thorough overhaul following the visit of the Union Home Minister and his top officials from Delhi. The IG of Police was replaced by S.K. Ghosh, a thoroughly competent and highly decorated police officer as the new Chief. The district administration was ruthlessly overhauled and erring officials from the Superintendent of Police downwards were identified, placed under suspension and proceeded against. The Government created a new Police Range and sanctioned contingents of armed police reserves to be stationed in selected vulnerable areas located far away from the District Headquarters. The package of reforms included new vehicles, improved means of communication, new buildings, additional manpower, arms and so on. The morale of the force took a quantum jump under the leadership of the new IG, who enjoyed the confidence and the backing of the Chief Minister Biju Patnaik, who was a go getter, no nonsense leader himself and dashing in every sense of the word. Within a short period, Orissa police assumed a new look and a much better image.

One afternoon in February 1965, I was summoned by the IG to meet him in his residential office. For the first five minutes, he explained that a young officer must not be wasted in Railway Police – a job better suited for an older person, who was about to retire. Then he broke the news. I would go to Sundargarh district and the present SP would be posted as SRP in my place from where he would retire soon. He then proceeded to narrate a terrifying account of all that needed to be done in the riot affected district in the coming months. The list included restoration of the confidence of members of the minority community in the police administration, expeditious investigation of several dozens of mass murders, looting and arson cases, completion of departmental proceedings against guilty police officers and so on. In fact, the IG dictated a note containing a list of about two dozen "do's" which I preserved for many years till that crumpled paper disappeared one day.

I took charge of the district on 24th February, 1965. It took me barely a month to find out that the 'babus' in the district police office ran their own empire and the subordinate police staff were completely at the mercy of the head clerk, the accountant and their minions in the police office and the Sub-Inspector in the Reserve Lines, commonly known as the "Line Babu". The pay and allowance of the force were often not sent till the 3rd week of the month causing enormous hardship to lower ranks and the constabulary in particular. Time and again, I discovered that cash rewards sanctioned months ago had not reached the concerned officer. Finally, one day things came to a head and I lost my temper. I threw the cash book across the table at the head clerk refusing to sign the monthly certificate when I discovered that pay and allowances had not been prepared and disbursed even after ten days of the month had passed. I raised my voice and the head clerk standing in front of me got a real earful.

That very afternoon, unknown to me, the entire ministerial staff held a secret meeting and sent petitions to the Chief Minister, Home Minister, the IG of Police and the Home Secretary levelling allegations of misbehaviour by an arrogant, ill-tempered IPS officer, who deserved to be sent out of the state as soon as possible. The IG thought it fit to ask the range DIG to look into this matter which the DIG did by paying a surprise visit to my Headquarters. I was asked to arrange a "durbar" at the Police Lines to be attended by all ranks present at the Headquarters as well as the clerks of the Police Office. I must admit that I did not find the proceedings palatable because it took me very little time to realize that I was defendant at the dock. But the meeting produced no surprise. The entire rank and file blamed the 'babus' in the police office for being unhelpful and mischievous. They demanded the transfer of the entire staff of the Police office. The objects of their anger, who were also present, listened to these outbursts in silence and obvious discomfort.

To this day, I do not know what my DIG wrote in his enquiry report. But he, before taking leave, gave me some sound advice. He said, "you will often have good reasons to lose your temper while dealing with your deviant subordinates. But take care to ensure that you do not throw things at the person standing in front of you or hurt his self-esteem by raising your voice beyond a point". He said that authority over subordinates can be exercised effectively by means other than angry outbursts. I found out in due course that it was better to remain calm outside, the more upset you got inside. The wise counsel of my senior stood me in good stead.

I learnt another lesson during the two years I spent in the district rather unexpectedly from a local social activist, who barged into my office one day with some complaint against the local police. During an exchange of argument, I had to remind him of the powers of the police and cautioned him to be careful. The old man looked me in the eye and said, "you enjoy absolutely no power *vis-a-vis* me or any other law-abiding citizen. You only have some limited powers over law breakers and common criminals". I have remembered these words till the end of my professional life.

The final incident I am about to relate is one which changed the way I saw people around me. The transformation in my way of looking at human beings shaped my attitude towards people in later years. I realised that many people have basic character ethics and qualities such as courage, loyalty and sense of duty which govern their actions and relations with individuals, irrespective of whether the other person has been nice or fair to him or not. When I first saw Reserve Inspector

Bimal Kumar Mohanty in Bolangir district, I was impressed by his smart athletic bearing. However, as time went by, his habit of taking things easy and delaying matters became a problem for which he had to be repeatedly censured by me. He was often caught on the wrong foot and on countless occasions, I had to tick him off. I have little doubt that as the Police Chief of Bolangir district, I had made his life miserable though he, no doubt, deserved all that he got. But how did he deal with his boss when he found himself one day in a truly extraordinary situation? The following summary from the report sent by the Government of Orissa recommending award of Prime Minister's "Medal for life saving" to the officer will speak for itself.

On 21st June, 1968, shortly after lunch, I received a phone message from the Sub-Divisional Officer that a leopard had appeared in Hirapur village under Luisingha Police Station and injured several persons. The villagers had left the village in panic and were requesting truck and car drivers passing by to inform the Collector and the SP so that immediate action could be taken to protect the villagers. My phone kept ringing as more and more such calls came from people, who met the distressed villagers on their way to the town. The Collector was out of station and so were the two Divisional Forest Officers. I had to do something. I initially thought of sending a small police party with the SDO to the village to organise the shooting of the leopard with the help of the villagers. On second thought, I felt that it would be inadvisable to let the matter be handled by them because indiscriminate or careless shooting might result in accidental injury or death of innocent villagers, which would worsen the situation. Hence, I decided to accompany the party.

On reaching the village, I learnt that the leopard had already been shot at from a distance by a local *shikari* following which the injured animal had escaped to a small forest at the end of the village. Not being a *shikari* myself, I made the blunder of my life and decided to enter the forest in search of the leopard with my inspector, who was full of enthusiasm. I took one constable, who happened to be the ace rifle shooter of the district. Inspector Mohanty had a .410 Musket and the two of us carried .303 rifles each. Without doubt the weapons were also singularly unsuited for hunting a leopard lying in wait for us inside a forest. Shortly after entering the bush, I was startled by a terrifying growl and saw the animal looking at me at a distance of about 20-25 feet. Before I could lift my rifle and press the trigger, it rushed towards me in a lightning burst of speed and pounced on me. The rifle was thrown away from my hand and I fell on the ground with my face up. As the animal charged at me, Inspector Mohanty, who had already fired at the rushing animal but missed it, came to my rescue. He repeatedly tried to hit the animal with the barrel of his empty gun and went on shouting to distract the animal.

After about a minute, the leopard which was trying to claw at me with one hand and snarling at Mohanty with the other, gave up and moved into a nearby bush. With the help of Mohanty, I got up bleeding in several parts of my body as a result of injuries inflicted by the clawing but otherwise miraculously safe and alive. The letter recommending the award ended thus: "But for the outstanding courage, presence of mind, loyalty and devotion to duty shown by Shri Bimal Kumar Mohanty, Shri Mitra might not have survived or in any event would have sustained very serious injuries. Had the Inspector displayed the normal human instinct of self-preservation and not rushed with an empty Musket to physically obstruct and ward off the injured animal in a desperate attempt to save the SP, then things would have been different". Mohanty was awarded the medal by Prime Minister Indira Gandhi during the All India Police Duty meet. Incidentally, constable Ghasiram Nanda, followed his natural instinct and as many others would have done in a similar situation, remained safely inactive behind a big tree nearby and watched the proceedings.

Later, I had occasion to ask Inspector Mohanty what prompted him to risk his life and face the injured animal with an empty gun. He said, "Sir, how could I leave you lying on the ground, with the animal charging at you ? I had to remain by your side, come what may". This young officer, who had to be given lessons by me day after day so that he could become a better and efficient police officer, apparently needed no lesson in basic character ethics and values which make human life worth living. These qualities are courage, sense of duty and loyalty. It was my turn to learn lessons of life from my junior colleague. "Obedience to duty, at all costs and risks, is the very essence of civilised life. Man does not live for himself alone". These were lines written by Samuel Smiles in 1880 and are as valid today as then.

13

Retrospection

VED MARWAH

I am against sermonising the young, because I believe that preaching has very little impact on the young minds and, in fact, can be counterproductive. Sometimes it invokes negative response even against sensible practical advice. This is especially true of our young officers, whose own personal experience can be very different from what they are being told. They cannot be blamed if they dismiss these lectures as impractical and hypocritical. I do not expect my young readers to become crusaders and sacrifice their careers for the sake of pursuing impractical ideas. But I wish to share my experience that success is possible even if one does not sacrifice one's principles and refuses to comply with the improper directions of the superiors. Many a time, our officers blame the political leaders or the 'system' for all the evils, but let me hasten to add that all political leaders cannot be tarred with the same brush. Most want the police to deliver on crime control and the maintenance of law and order. Even a most difficult political leader has little respect for an inefficient and corrupt police officer. And at times, a temporary setback can turn out to be a blessing in the long run. Do not worry too much about your career. Even in the current political system, there is a huge space available for professional and committed police officers.

True, things have changed for the worse in recent years, but it would be a gross exaggeration to say that a police career depends solely on the politicians. So-called failures or successes in one's career depend on many factors, and most of them are not under one's control. Following the path of least resistance cannot always ensure success. The number of those who have suffered in their careers because they did not comply with the illegal orders is much smaller than those who tried to advance their careers by currying favour with the politicians. In any case, a study of career profiles of the so-called successful police officers will show that their career graph is dependent on the interplay of many factors and all of them had their quota of ups and downs. As I look back at my own career, I come more and more to the conclusion that it was my professional stand as a police officer that contributed most to the development of my career. The most coveted posts in my career came to me on their own and not because I craved for them.

The most challenging assignment in my entire police career was the job of the Commissioner of Police, Delhi. Let me describe how I got this job. For some time I was out of the police department and serving as a Joint Secretary incharge of women's development in the Union Ministry of Social Welfare. On October 31, 1984, when Mrs. Indira Gandhi was assassinated, I was in Jaipur attending a meeting with the Secretary, Social Welfare, Rajasthan, and his officers to review the development programmes for women in Rajasthan. The meeting had to be ended abruptly when this terrible news reached us. All the offices of the Government of Rajasthan were immediately closed down as a mark of respect to the late Prime Minister. It was apparent that things were not going to be normal for quite some time. Therefore, I decided to leave Jaipur and return to Delhi. I requested my liaison officer to book me by the next flight for Delhi. Within a few minutes, however, my liaison officer told me that there was absolutely no chance of getting a seat in the flight to Delhi, because of huge rush of VIPs, like ministers and political leaders, wanting to go to Delhi. I was advised to take my chance in a bus which was leaving the next morning. I decided to board the bus not realising what I was in for. It was a long and torturous journey which took almost two days to reach Delhi. Even then I considered myself lucky that I made it because we had to face serious trouble on the way from Jaipur to Delhi at many places. We reached Delhi around ten at night the next day. In Delhi, the scene was much worse. The whole city was in turmoil. Serious riots had erupted in Delhi and there was no question of any transport being available. There was no alternative but to walk all the way with my baggage, mercifully light, from the inter-state bus stand to my house at Lodhi Estate. For the next few days, it appeared that the whole city was on fire. The Delhi Police was not visible on most Delhi roads. Small crowds of anti-social elements took over the city and were burning Sikhs and their properties at will. The Delhi Police came under very severe criticism. It took more than a week for the city to return to some sort of normalcy. The people were feeling very insecure and this sense of insecurity was not confined only to the Sikhs. The anti-social elements had also started targeting the property of the well-to-do members of other communities in some residential colonies. It appeared as if the whole law and order machinery in the city had broken down.

I could go to my office at Shastri Bhavan only after a week to prepare some papers in connection with a conference that I had to attend in Singapore. It was in the office that I received a call from Shri Arun Singh, an aide to the PM Shri Rajiv Gandhi asking me to immediately come to the Prime Minister's house to meet the Prime Minister. I immediately rushed to the PM's house at 1 Safdarjung Road and was ushered into Mr. Arun Singh's room. He had a long chat with me about the Delhi Police. To cut a long story short, I was told by the Prime Minister that a decision had been taken to bring me back to the Delhi Police to restore its confidence and morale. I left the Prime Minister's house with an understanding that I was being appointed as the Commissioner of Police. However, to my utter amazement, when the orders came I was appointed as the Additional Commissioner, CID, in IG's rank in the newly created post. Shri S.S. Jog from the Maharashtra cadre was appointed as the new Commissioner of Police. I contacted Shri Arun Singh once again and expressed my disappointment at my being posted as an Additional Commissioner. An officer junior to me, Shri P.S. Bhinder, had already held the Commissioner's job years back. I was, however, given no option and asked to join the new post as an Additional Commissioner of Police. In addition to my job in the CID department, I was also appointed as the Inquiry Officer to enquire into the role of the Delhi Police during the riot after Mrs. Gandhi's assassination. You can appreciate my disappointment that though I was the seniormost UT cadre officer, I was not only deprived of the job that being a cadre post should have come to me, but was entrusted with the unenviable task of enquiring against my own colleagues. I went about the task of enquiry in as objective a manner as possible. On the positive side, I found Shri Jog a very upright and straightforward boss to work with. We were getting along quite well when a personal tragedy struck Shri Jog. His wife, who was in the best of health, was diagnosed as a cancer patient during a routine medical test. Shri Jog was heart broken and wanted to leave his Delhi post immediately. He first went on leave to get his wife admitted in a hospital in Bombay and then requested the Government for his reversion to his state. All these developments took place within four months of Shri Jog's arrival in Delhi. During Shri Jog's absence from Delhi I was asked to look after the job of the Delhi Police Commissioner and everyone took it for granted that with the acceptance of Shri Jog's request for reversion to his parent cadre Maharashtra, I would be appointed in his place. But that was not to be ! Government in its wisdom decided to appoint Shri J.F. Ribeiro, also of Maharashtra cadre, as the next Police Commissioner. Shri Ribeiro, however, applied for leave to attend to some of his personal problems before taking over his new assignment in Delhi. I was to continue as the acting Delhi Police Commissioner till his arrival.

It was during that period that Delhi was hit with transistor bombs by the Sikh terrorists who wanted to take revenge for the 1984 riots in Delhi. More than 50 persons were killed and many more injured. The people of Delhi were furious. The media had screaming headlines not only against me, but also against the young Prime Minister Rajiv Gandhi. They demanded my immediate removal and the resignation of the Prime Minister. You can imagine my unenviable position. On the one hand, I had to face the anger of the Prime Minister and the Union Home Minister; and on the other, the wrath of the

Delhi public, and I was only an acting Commissioner of Police. I had reconciled to my fate and I knew that my head was on the chopping line, when a miracle of miracles happened. The then Deputy Commissioner of Central District, Shri Amod Kanth, came to see me to share with me an information that Delhi lawyer's house was suspected to be the place where these transistor bombs were being assembled. It was decided that before searching the eminent lawyer's house, a watch should be kept over it for confirmation of the information. The surveillance team confirmed the information and a raid was organized on the advocate's house. He and some of the co-conspirators with explosive materials and bomb-making equipments were apprehended red-handed and they made a clean confession to the police. Search parties were organised in different parts of the city to raid the hiding places of all those involved in this criminal conspiracy. The whole gang was neutralised and the Delhi newspapers, which were baying for my blood, overnight became my strong admirers and supporters. The Delhi public heaved a sigh of relief as the transistor bomb explosions stopped with the neutralisation of this gang. Prime Minister Rajiv Gandhi personally rang me up to congratulate me on the Delhi Police success. Apparently, to reward me the Government decided to appoint Shri Ribeiro as DGP, CRPF and I was appointed in his place as the Delhi Police Commissioner. The job came to me because, rightly or wrongly, I had earned the reputation of being a professional officer who did not compromise on principles. I had little personal contribution in the successful working out of this important case and yet the circumstances combined in a manner which gave me the credit.

This is not the only occasion when circumstances, some may call it fate, intervened in my favour. And, of course, sometimes it was the reverse. One has to accept the good with the bad and take life as it comes. Twice in my service career for over one year I was without any posting on what is euphemistically called compulsory waiting ! On the other hand, years after retiring from police service, I was in Bern in Switzerland in November 1999, when I got a telephone call from the Home Minister Shri L.K. Advani offering me the post of Manipur Governor. I was surprised when this offer was made to me because I had retired from the service eight years ago and was not under consideration for a job like this. Therefore, there was no question of any *quid pro quo* for the services rendered to the politicians. When I called on Shri Advani on my return to Delhi and asked him how my name had cropped up for this job, he told me that they had decided to appoint someone to the post who had not canvassed for it. This is how I became the Governor of Manipur.

If we look at the career profiles of officers who have secured an appointment by kowtowing to the political masters, then it will be seen that they have not always done very well in that coveted post. Even those politicians, who ask you to do a wrong thing, do not respect you for complying with their illegal directions. Politicians are shrewd and they are quick to assess an officer whether he would oblige them or not. All upright and professional officers may not have done always very well, but an unprofessional and spineless officer has invariably not done well. No one can really guide you when to assert yourself and when not to, as the judgment is yours and yours alone. Based on my experience, I can only say that a straight and professional path is not only a sound one but is a more rewarding one in the long run.

Professionalism is really the key to a successful career. Police officers are called upon to take the leadership role right from the beginning of their career, and that role they cannot discharge if they are not sound professionals in their job. A thorough knowledge of law, investigation, police rules and traits like physical and moral courage are absolutely essential for a successful police career. Though some might have got the job because of their succumbing to illegal demands, they do not make very happy police officers. They are not respected by their own subordinates and are ridiculed by the peer group. It is too big a cost to pay for any job. Ridiculed by their subordinates and colleagues and bullied by their seniors, they make pathetic officers, unhappy in their jobs and not very happy in their dealings with others. This is not to say that one will not have to face rough weather when one takes a principled stand. But then there are compensations also for taking a professional line.

It is only professionalism that can earn one the respect of one's subordinates and colleagues. And subordinates' loyalty is a very useful asset to have. It has come to my rescue more than once when I was in trouble. Let me relate the story when the Union Home Minister got annoyed with me for some reasons when I was the Commissioner of Police, Delhi. He was looking for an opportunity to settle scores with me for not obliging him. And that opportunity came after an unfortunate incident when my driver drove in from the opposite direction as the Russian Prime Minister's cavalcade approached Rashtrapati Bhavan. Prime Minister Rajiv Gandhi, who was travelling with the Russian Prime Minister, saw my car. He was annoyed, but this should not have been a reason enough to take the extreme step of sacking me uncere-moniously. I was rung at midnight by the Minister of State to inform me that the Government had decided to sack me and that I should apply for leave. Unbelievable, but this is how it happened to a Delhi Police Commissioner. But what followed was even more unbelievable. The entire media, all ranks of Delhi Police and the Delhi public came to my support against the order of the Government. The Government gave in to the tremendous public pressure and I was asked to cut short the leave and report back to my old job. Even persons at the highest level hesitate to play rough shod over you when your force is on your side.

The biggest resource the police department has is the human resource. Subordinate ranks are the cutting edge in the police department. It is mostly they who interact with the people. Do not neglect them. Look after them and listen to them. The growing distance between the junior ranks needs to be reduced. They are a storehouse of information and are gifted with shrewd commonsense. True, everyone is not the same; there are good officers and not so good officers. But time and again, I have found that a well-knit team can do wonders. Some are good at investigations and others for law and order duties.

It is important to discriminate and make use of them according to their capabilities. The best among them are like race horses who need skilful riders. I have no hesitation in saying that I have learnt more from them than from my seniors. Earn their respect and trust, and this can be an invaluable asset. I can never forget late Inspector Godha Ram and Dy. SP A.C. Tuli, two of the finest investigating officers I have come across in my career. Both possessed an uncanny sixth sense which bailed me out from very difficult situations.

One such situation came up when I was DIG Range in the Delhi Police (Those days there was only one DIG Range). Wife of a well-known eye surgeon Dr. Jain, on whom only a few days before the incident, Padmashri award had been conferred, was murdered right in front of their house in Defence Colony in the evening when Dr. and Mrs. Jain were about to get into their car. You can imagine the public outrage. The Delhi Police was already facing a lot of public criticism because of a number of robberies that had taken place in South Delhi. Dr. Jain was also the Hony. Surgeon to the President. No less persons than the President and the Prime Minister wanted to know about the progress of the case. I was in deep trouble. And it was then that Tuli and Ashok Patel, another brilliant investigator, broke the conspiracy behind this crime. After sustained interrogation, it was discovered that Dr. Jain himself had hired an assassin from Rajasthan to commit the murder of his wife. Dr. Jain was convicted and all his appeals rejected. A committed team with high degree of integrity and professionalism can do wonders ! There will always be bad hats in a team, but a well-knit team can successfully face all the challenges. The good work of the subordinate ranks must be publicly recognised and the tendency by some senior officers to hog all the limelight should be discouraged. It is the leader's main task to motivate the team.

It is not always understood that accountability of the police is not confined only to its own hierarchical structure. The police is directly accountable to the people, for whom it provides the essential service of protection of life and property, and as it enforces the rule of law, to the judiciary, apart from their own superiors and political bosses. The media and public leaders exercise indirect control over the functioning of the police. An effective and successful police officer keeps in close touch with all of them. The difficulty arises when there are conflicting demands, especially, because the police exercises a lot of discretion in performing its role. At times, it is tight rope walking, but at all times it is useful to remember that the police has to function within the parameters of law. Discretion should be exercised in favour of the weaker sections and not in favour of the rich and the well-to-do.

In this brief article, I have touched upon only a few issues. To sum up, young officers should not unduly worry about how their career will shape in the future. If you are on the right track, the future will take care of itself. Ups and downs are part of life. Eventually, everyone has to believe in himself and his destiny. Police is a profession and the days of generalist police officer are over. A successful officer has to acquire professional skills and the qualities of leadership alongwith a sense of commitment to public service. This is not an impractical, idealistic advice, but sound and practical advice. Ultimately, it is you and you alone who are going to decide how you are going to function. Blaming others or even the system will not serve your interests, if you desire a successful career.

14

Remembrance of Things Small and Significant

CHAMAN LAL

I was Superintendent of Police, Shivpuri (MP), when the Janata party Government of Morarji Desai, which came to power in July, 1977 after defeating Indira Gandhi, constituted a Commission of Enquiry to look into the excesses of Emergency. Justice J.C. Shah, a retired Judge of the Supreme Court, comprised the one man Commission. Mr. P.R. Rajagopal, an officer of the First Batch (1948) of the IPS belonging to MP cadre was appointed as Secretary. Mr. Rajagopal, recipient of Padmashri for his commendable services as the Chief of BSF Intelligence in 1971 war, was widely known for his competence, courage and integrity and enjoyed the enviable distinction of being one of the favourites of Mr. K.F. Rustamji.

I joined the Shah Commission on September 9, 1977, in compliance with the orders issued by the MP Government on receipt of a wireless message from Mr. Rajagopal. Although he had left MP on deputation to BSF before I joined the cadre, I had heard so much about his professional talents, personal integrity and leadership qualities. He was second only to Mr. K.F. Rustamji in moulding my professional beliefs and shaping my work style. He was soft to the extent of being indulgent towards sincere and hardworking subordinates, who might otherwise be just mediocre in their performance and results. The other category of clever, cunning and corrupt could never impress him, despite their achievements and successes.

Mr. Rajagopal had inspired and guided me to my most cherished belief that only a truly honest civil servant endowed with a reasonably good measure of ability and capacity for hard work can afford the luxury of fearlessness and enjoy the privilege of being at peace with himself. I was fortunate to have been spotted by him while working as an ASP in Gwalior and nurtured by him in his image of a police officer.

I began my first day in the Shah Commission with calling on Justice Shah, a simple, soft spoken and reserved man with an irresistible charm and saintly elegance. True to his reputation of being a man of few words, he dismissed me in no time by asking me to receive briefing about my work from Mr. Rajagopal.

As secretary of the Commission, Mr. Rajagopal was its Chief Executive Officer. He was the kingpin of the Commission processing all matters, legal, administrative and financial which were put up to Justice Shah for final orders. The most demanding and laborious job of the Secretary was to scrutinise the complaints which were pouring in thousands from all over the country. Complaints were prioritised in accordance with the gravity of the allegations and the urgency of relief sought by the victims. A lot of material was required to be collected from the authorities concerned before the case could be put up to the Commission for hearing as per the procedure decided by Justice Shah following the provisions of the Commission of Enquiry Act 1955.

Mr. Rajagopal briefed me in detail about the complaint handling procedure and assigned me an important area of civil liberties – abuse of MISA during Emergency. I was instructed to investigate in detail some specific cases of detention under MISA pertaining to Delhi. Only a few of these were based on specific petitions received from or on behalf of the victims. Most of the cases were selected by the Commission by taking *suo motu* cognisance of the media reports about excesses of Emergency in Delhi. I was later involved in preparing comprehensive reports on the abuse of powers under MISA in UP, Bihar, MP, West Bengal, Andhra Pradesh, Karnataka, Punjab, Haryana, J&K, Mizoram and A&N Islands. My designation was OSD and my work was supervised by Mr. S.K. Sharma, DIG (IPS: 1958 Rajasthan), a close associate with the shared background of BSF and commonality of values and commitments.

Work in the Commission would begin every morning with an address by the Secretary to all the senior and middle level officers. Mr. Rajagopal was a firm believer in the power and obligation of the leader to motivate the senior staff to give of their best and inspire the subordinates with personal example. He was fond of describing himself as a slave driver in making us obtain our goals, though most of us exchanged smiles whenever this word was uttered. Even his worst critics agreed that genuine concern for the comfort and welfare of the subordinates was the most striking characteristic of Mr. Rajagopal's work style. He never felt tired of reminding us about the "purity of means" in our investigations into sensitive cases. He would tell us that we were chosen to be associated with the sacred task of presenting to the people of the country, a truthful account of what had happened during the Emergency. Mr. Rajagopal cautioned us against the pitfalls of over-enthusiasm and lack of objectivity in our reporting and taught us to shun publicity. He used to reiterate as an article of faith every morning our obligation to adhere to the principles of natural justice and give the accused persons every possible opportunity to present his/her version of the matter under inquiry. We were instructed to consider dispassionately every piece of relevant information encountered by us without bothering to see whether it supported or refuted our line of investigation and include it in our report. He also guarded us against the tempting tendency of trying to fix the powerful functionaries in administration and politics, who had earned the wrath of the people and enmity of their colleagues because of their arrogant ways in the days of emergency.

My tenure in the Shah Commission of Enquiry proved very rewarding in refining my investigative abilities and sharpening my analytical skills. My work, particularly, the detention cases of Delhi, brought me into close contact with some of the mighty public figures of emergency, LG Krishan Chand, his Secretary,

Naveen Chawla whom he described as the Governor Delhi, Mrs. Gandhi's closest confidant R.K. Dhawan, Sanjay Gandhi's henchman DIG Police, P.S. Bhinder and DM Sushil Kumar, who was exposed by the *Indian Express* for handing over blank but duly signed MISA detention forms to the police authorities. Almost all the ADMs and Supdts. of Police of Delhi figured in my cases which were heard publicly by the Commission and received wide coverage by national and international media. Arun Shouri, the emerging hero of investigative journalism brought out a series of edit page articles in the *Indian Express*. Someone remarked that "Delhi was taken by storm by these exposures which revealed direct involvement of PM, Mrs. Gandhi; MoS, Om Mehta; LG, Krishan Chand; and top officers of civil administration in the excesses of emergency. Mr. Karl Khandalwal and Mr. P.N. Lekhi, Commission's Counsel were doing a marvellous job in projecting before the Commission the true face of emergency reconstructed from the accounts of victims.

My first presentation was the detention of Mr. Bhim Sen Sachar, veteran freedom fighter, who was former CM, Punjab and India's High Commissioner in Sri Lanka. I could prove to the satisfaction of the Commission that his detention under MISA, and immediate transfer to Ambala jail was linked to a letter he had addressed to Mrs. Gandhi, jointly with seven other prominent Gandhians. The author of this letter, which formed the grounds of their detention under MISA, had denounced the imposition of emergency and reminded Mrs. Gandhi about the constitutional rights of the people of India under the democratic edifice built so assiduously by the great leaders of our freedom struggle, including her own father, India's first Prime Minister Jawaharlal Nehru. She was advised to accept dissent and criticism as essential components of democracy, revoke emergency and set free Morarji Desai, JP and several others, who were in prison simply for having opposed Indira Gandhi's continuance in power after the Allahabad High Court verdict against her. Mr. Bhim Sen Sachar's case was followed by the case of Mr. Prabir Purkayastha, a student of Jawaharlal Nehru University, who was picked up by police at the instance of Mrs. Maneka Gandhi and turned out to be a case of mistaken identity. He remained in jail till the end of emergency. Detention of Promila Lewis, a social activist, Arun Jaitley, student leader of Delhi, were among the 7-8 cases I had presented before the Commission.

I recall the case of one Mr. Shukla, who was detained under MISA simply for addressing a petition to LG Delhi about the detention of his brother, who was a Professor and had come to adverse notice for his political views. There was another pathetic case of detention under MISA of a young boy, an ordinary thief, who got caught in the police drive to make Delhi crime-free during emergency.

There was a set pattern in all the cases of detention that I studied from the files of Delhi Administration to select some representative cases. The detention order signed by the District Magistrate was invariably based on an unverified police report accusing the person concerned of some subversive activity attracting the provisions of the Maintenance of Internal Security Act (MISA). The grounds of detention were recorded in a crude and ludicrous manner accusing the poor man of trying to overthrow the Government of Mrs. Gandhi by raising anti-emergency slogans near a railway station or bus stand. In most cases, the victim was first arrested under section 108/151 Cr.PC and thereafter served with the detention order MISA. Once in jail, he remained there, deprived of all constitutional and legal rights of bail, remission and parole. The term of detention initially fixed as 6 months was mechanically extended in a heartless manner just by initiating a note and getting the signatures of the Lt. Governor. In quite a few cases, the final orders on the file were passed by the Secretary to the LG recording that the LG had approved the extension.

I worked out my own procedure of preparing a case for presentation before the Commission and got it duly approved by the Secretary. I would first make a summary of the case giving all relevant facts and figures of the detention from the initial arrest till the final release of the detenue. Then followed the questioning of the SP and ADM concerned to verify the police report and detention orders. I would thereafter record the statements of the officers whom I found very candid and straight in most cases. They felt no hesitation and found it in their interest to state truthfully the background of each case. In all the cases which I had selected for presentation, orders for detention had originated from 'high-ups'. The names of R.K. Dhawan and P.S. Bhinder figured prominently in all my cases. R.K. Dhawan was the most powerful PS to the Prime Minister that this country has ever known. Mr. P.S. Bhinder, DIG of Police was *de facto* chief of Delhi Police, partly, because of his proximity to Sanjay Gandhi, but largely due to the willing surrender of authority by the IGP, Mr. Bhawani Mal. I tried but failed to persuade the high profile dignitaries to give me their version of the cases in which they were named by the district officials. Mr. Bhinder was always cool and composed and told me politely that he would state whatever he had to say before the Commission. Mr. Dhawan took the same stand and looked confident to explain everything. After discussing the broad details with my DIG, Mr. S.K. Sharma, I made narrative of each case mentioning the facts of detention, evidence collected from the statements of officials and the list of witnesses to be produced before the Commission. The hearing of the case by the Commission would commence with a reading of the narrative of the case by me, followed by the appearance of officers, whose statements I had recorded. Thereafter, Mr. P.S. Bhinder, Mr. R.K. Dhawan, Mr. Naveen Chawla and Mr. Krishan Chand would be called one by one to answer questions arising from the deposition before the Commission. The questions were framed by Justice Shah himself. Mrs. Gandhi was also summoned in the case of detention of Mr. Bhimsen Sachar. She, however, defied the summon in this as well as several other cases and involved the Commission in a legal wrangle.

All my cases were listed together and were heard on day to day basis over a period of 5-6 days. Three-four days were taken by the appearance of SPs and ADMs. They confirmed the statement recorded by me and produced some additional facts which they thought could help them by highlighting the peculiar environment and culture in which they were made to work during emergency. Justice Shah realised their helplessness because of their relatively low place in the hierarchy and was, therefore, rarely harsh while telling them plainly that they had failed in discharging their constitutional duties and obligations and were wrong in exercising their powers arbitrarily under the mistaken belief that "orders from above" can be an acceptable plea. Mr. Bhinder's deposition did not take much time as he was like R.K. Dhawan, one of the few, who readily accepted all blame without bringing in any political figure – MoS (Home) or Mrs. Gandhi. Mr. Naveen Chawla faced the Commission coolly explaining with confidence his role as Secretary to LG and attributing all decisions right or wrong to his boss.

Every SP had mentioned Mr. Bhawani Mal, IGP Delhi, in his statement and stated directly or implicitly that the IGP had willingly allowed his deputy Mr. Bhinder, DIG, to function as *de facto* IGP and make Delhi Police the handmaiden of Sanjay Gandhi, the kingpin of emergency. Although I had not recorded the statement of Mr. Bhawani Mal as he did not figure directly in any case of detention, I had included his name in the list of persons, who were required to appear before the Commission and give evidence on matters involving them which found mention in the statements of district officers. Mr. Bhawani Mal was summoned to appear before the Commission after the deposition of the SPs., ADMs and DIG Bhinder was over. One session was exclusively earmarked for his deposition.

It was around 5 PM on the day preceding the date of Mr. Bhawani Mal's appearance before the Commission, I was informed by my DIG S.K. Sharma that the Commission had decided to exempt Mr. Bhawani Mal from appearance the following morning and I should accordingly prepare myself for the deposition of the next witness on the list. I learnt that Mr. Bhawani Mal had seen Mr. Rajagopal, a few minutes back and the decision to spare him the ordeal of explaining his role in emergency to the Commission was taken on his personal request to Mr. Rajagopal, who was his batch-mate in service and a close friend of many years. The news upset me terribly. I had painstakingly woven the record of MISA detentions in

Delhi by incorporating the versions of the various functionaries in a logical sequence, convincingly building the charge of abuse of powers by the district officers at the behest of the political masters. Every link in this account had its specific significance and Mr. Bhawani Mal formed one of the crucial links whose exclusion at that late stage could seriously dilute the force of my findings.

I sought an appointment with Mr. Rajagopal. Within a few minutes, I was ushered into his room. Mr. Rajagopal could always read my mind easily, particularly, when I was tense and agitated for some reason. He could sense the disturbed state of my mind and enquired lovingly what had happened. I asked him straightaway whether it was true that Mr. Bhawani Mal had been exempted from appearance before the Commission in my cases fixed for the following day. He said 'yes' and looked at me rather sternly to see my reaction. I said in an angry tone, "Sir, he is an important witness in my cases. The cases which you know I have constructed with a great deal of difficulty exposing myself to some personal risk. Don't you think, sir, that I should have been consulted before such a major decision was taken".

Mr. Rajagopal was, to all of us, the undisputed boss of the Commission. Our work seldom brought us face to face with Justice Shah except during the hearing when he presided over the Commission with Mr. Rajagopal sitting next to him and we read out our reports. Every decision concerning our work, whether administrative or legal, used to come to us from Mr. Rajagopal. It was, therefore, very natural for him to get angry when I questioned his decision regarding the appearance of Mr. Bhawani Mal. He told me in a sharp and bossy tone which I had never known before that he had taken the decision after careful consideration of the matter from all angles and I need not worry myself on that count. His claim that he had decided to exempt Mr. Bhawani Mal from appearance after considering the matter in detail infuriated me further. I said, "Sir, you know what all the SPs and ADMs have stated about Mr. Bhawani Mal. These young officers, who are helping us in knowing the truth about the days of emergency, have blamed

Mr. Bhawani Mal for abdicating his powers and responsibilities and choosing to following the convenient course of allowing Mr. Bhinder to run Delhi Police. How can we use this important evidence in our final findings without giving Mr. Bhawani Mal a chance to confirm or deny his total surrender through silence or inaction ? One thing more, sir are we not morally bound to provide some protection and relief to these young officers by letting the public know as to how their superiors had functioned during emergency" ?

Mr. Rajagopal had always known my independence and fearlessness in matters of conviction. I had earned his generous praise for these qualities in my encounters with the politicians and superiors in service. Still, he could not tolerate my open vehement opposition to one of his decisions whose full implications he was, at that moment, unwilling to appreciate. He got from his seat in anger and shouted at me, "I have heard you enough. You must not forget that you are an OSD in the rank of SP. I am the Secretary of the Commission and it is for me to decide such matters. Mr. Bhawani Mal explained to me his personal difficulties and I have taken this decision. If there are any adverse implications to your case, you take care of them. Let me tell you today what I have never told you before. You are a difficult person for those above you, You may be popular among your subordinates but everybody above you, including your DIG in the Commission, is unhappy with you because of your rigid attitude and arrogant behaviour".

I felt hurt by Mr. Rajagopal's remarks describing me a difficult person. I knew I had never been popular with my bosses because of my strict and passionate attachment to my view point in everything. But I sincerely believed that I had never been rude or arrogant. I could see that I had placed Mr. Rajagopal in a difficult situation and his anger was justified.

I left Mr. Rajagopal probably without taking leave and returned to my room. I felt totally shaken and disheartened. I hurriedly collected all the files and papers from the tables and put them in the almirah and went out for my standard cure for the tormented mind– an unplanned long and lonely walk of several hours.

I cannot recall the precise stage in my professional career when I had discovered the most efficacious cure for my emotional disturbances of serious but temporary nature. I would drop everything and go out on a long walk preferably to some quiet corner of the city. I would walk for hours at slow pace and in small steps inwardly talking to myself over the issue that had upset me. Sometimes, I would utter something aloud inviting suspicious looks from the passersby. I would engage myself in an animated dialogue with my adversary and advance argument after argument to counter his possible points. I would invariably return triumphant from the struggle, calm and peaceful, totally convinced of the correctness of my stand and happy with myself for having protested against what I had found unacceptable.

The long walk, taking me from Patiala House to the end of Janpath, then back to Tilak Bridge and finally to Minto Road Hostel via Deen Dayal Upadhyay Marg, produced the desired effect. I felt that I was absolutely right. I congratulated myself for having protested against Mr. Rajagopal's decision. At the same time, I could also appreciate his angry reaction and the remarks about myself being a difficult person. I told myself that I had driven him beyond his threshold of tolerance and his anger was totally justified. I decided I would make a formal submission to the Commission not to close these cases without questioning Mr. Bhawani Mal.

It was past 9 p.m. when I entered my flat in the Tagore Hostel Apartment. I found Ma terribly worried by my long absence and the repeated calls on telephone she had been receiving since 7 PM. She told me that Mr. Rajagopal had called 3-4 times and there were calls from the Control Room also. She scolded me in her characteristic sweet way for my habit of disappearing from others like this. Just then the telephone rang. It was Inspector Faulkner, Incharge Control Room. His voice betrayed a sense of relief on finding me. He told me that he was trying to locate me ever since I had left the office. The Control Room van had been going up and down all possible paths of my evening walk which most of my colleagues knew was an essential part of my daily routine. Inspector Faulkner told me that Mr. Rajagopal had called for me a few minutes after I left his room and was desperately trying to contact me. He had instructed the Control Room to trace me and ask me to speak to him immediately.

I rang up Mr. Rajagopal at his residence number. He picked up the phone. I said, "Good evening sir, it is Chaman. I was informed by the Control Room that you wanted me to speak to you". I don't think he heard me fully. He said in a tone that was eager but calm, "Chaman, I am sorry. I was unfair to you this evening. You are right. We cannot do without Mr. Bhawani Mal's evidence. He will appear before the Commission tomorrow. He has been informed".

I felt happy over the unexpected development and was touched by the magnanimity of Mr. Rajagopal whom I had offended with my impetuous conduct a few hours back. I said in an apologetic tone, "Sir, thank you very much. Please forgive me for my impertinence of this evening". He replied in a softer and loving tone, "no Chaman, you were right in your opinion, even though your manner of expressing it could be questioned. What ultimately matters is the rightness of the stand we take in a certain situation. That is why it is me who should apologise, not you".

Mr. Rajagopal used to introduce me to his intimate friends as 'my third son' and I was fond of addressing him as "*Appa*" outside the office hours. In that emotionally charged state of mind, I could not restrain myself from saying, "Appa, thank you very much for your understanding and kindness".

Mr. Bhawani Mal appeared before the Commission on the following morning. I had prepared a set of questions and flagged the relevant portions from the statements of the SPs and the ADMs for his examination by the Commission. Justice Shah added a few more queries. The Commission's counsellors P.N. Lekhi and Khandalwal had several questions to ask. Mr. Frank Anthony, Mrs. Gandhi's counsellor, who was also defending Mr. R.K. Dhawan, had hardly anything to say. Mr. Bhawani Mal's statement before the Commission was credited with great evidentiary value and high credibility. The Police Chief of the nation's capital informed the whole world about the working of the inner coterie, the 'charmed circle' of the emergency. Mr. R.K. Dhawan used to hold daily morning meetings at Mrs. Gandhi's residence which was attended by the L.G. Krishan Chand, his Secretary Naveen Chawla, DM Sushil Kumar and DIG P.S. Bhinder. Events of the previous 24 hours were discussed and plans for the day were formulated. One never knew how much of what these levers of emergency decided and did, was actually known to Mrs. Gandhi. Mr. Bhawani Mal's statement was widely covered by the media. I recall the 9 o'clock evening news of the AIR had said that "everything went awry during emergency, says the former Chief of Police, Delhi".

15

An Unforgettable Experience

F.T.R. COLASO

The most difficult law and order situation I had to face in my career, spanning almost 35 years in the police, was very early in my career, as a young Superintendent of Police.

I had been promoted as Supdt. of Police in June 1965, soon after my marriage, and was posted as SP of Chitradurga in Karnataka. At that time, newly promoted officers were posted to comparatively smaller districts which were also considered to be not too problematic. Chitradurga was considered to be one such. For almost a year after I took charge, it remained so. While the district headquarters, Chitradurga, was a small town having a population of about 50,000, there was a bigger town in the district, Davangere and a nearby satellite town of Harihar, with a combined population of about 1.5 lakhs and at a distance of just 25 kms. from each other. Davangere itself was 40 kms. away from Chitradurga.

Sometime in June 1966, the boundary dispute between Karnataka and Maharashtra over Belgaum and other areas bordering Maharashtra, which had been simmering for many years after the Mahajan Commission had given its report, suddenly erupted and agitations began in the northern districts of Karnataka, particularly in Belgaum and Dharwad, which spread to Harihar and Davangere, which are bordering Dharwad district. The agitation took place mainly along the railway line connecting Poona and Bangalore via Miraj, Belgaum, Dharwad, Hubli, Harihar and Davangere.

I received information one day in June 1966 that the trains running between Poona and Bangalore were going to be stopped at Harihar and Davangere as a token protest by the agitators demanding implementation of the Mahajan Commission recommendations. The information available at the time was that the proposed demonstration would be only a token one in which the protestors would stop the trains at Harihar and Davangere for about 10 to 15 minutes and then allow them to proceed. The intelligence available also indicated that the number of protestors at each place would be only about a hundred.

Accordingly, necessary police *bandobast* was made in the light of the intelligence available. It is also relevant to mention that at that time the strength of the entire District Armed Reserve consisted of only 6 platoons with a total strength of about 200 personnel. Even this small strength was divided between the district headquarters of Chitradurga and Davangere with the latter having a strength of less than 100.

After receipt of the information about the proposed agitation, I left for Davangere alongwith my wife in my own private car as those days the Supdts. of Police were only provided with jeeps which were old and not in good condition. After arriving at Davangere in the afternoon and arranging for my wife to be accommodated in the local Inspection Bungalow situated close to the Davangere Extension Police Station, I went over to the office of the local S.D.P.O. which is situated in the same building, to ascertain the latest information about the agitation and plan for police arrangements to be made for the following morning when, as per information received, the Bangalore-Miraj Express passing through Harihar would be stopped by the agitators.

Accordingly, early next morning I went to Harihar alongwith a contingent of Armed Police, consisting of hardly 25 as that was the number available due to the very inadequate strength of the District Armed Reserve. A small number of Civil Police Officers and other ranks comprising about 15 made up the total number of policemen available to deal with the proposed agitation. This force was deployed at Harihar railway station where the Express train from Bangalore to Miraj was due to pass through at about 9 a.m. The train duly arrived at the scheduled time. A group of agitators numbering about 100 had also assembled and as soon as the train stopped, they squatted on the railway line in front of the engine and declared that they would not permit the train to proceed. They had earlier given an assurance that they would stop the train for only about 15 to 20 minutes more than the scheduled stop as a token protest. However, the leaders now declared that they would stop the train for an indefinite period and would not allow it to proceed unless the Chief Minister himself came from Bangalore to assure them that their demands would be conceded. They further made several absurd and unacceptable demands. No amount of arguments and requests to be reasonable, as they were putting innocent passengers to considerable inconvenience, had any effect on them. Meanwhile I had sent word to the local Deputy Commissioner of the district, who was also the District Magistrate and who was attending a meeting at Harihar, to come to the station as the situation was getting out of hand and his presence was required to deal with the situation. Instead of coming to the spot, he sent the local Tahsildar, who evidently was not in a position to deal with the situation and went back to the DM to apprise him of the seriousness of the situation and ask him to come himself, but even then the DM failed to respond.

In the meantime, the passengers in the train and the railway authorities were growing restless as already almost 2 hours had passed since the train had been stopped. They complained about police inaction and wanted me to do something about it. Finding that the DM was not likely to come to deal with the situation and in fact was avoiding coming, I felt I had to act. Accordingly, I told the leaders of the agitation that they had stopped the train sufficiently long and that if they did not move away from the railway line and allow the train to proceed, I would have to arrest and prosecute them. They responded by becoming more defiant. In the meantime, the crowd had swelled to over a thousand and was growing in numbers.

After issuing a final warning, I proceeded to arrest the

persons squatting on the railway track. There were about a dozen of them surrounded by another 100 or so. When we tried to take the arrested persons, they clung on to the rails and kept kicking and shouting. A scuffle ensued and the mob became violent and started pelting stones on the police. There were plenty of granite stones on and near the railway track which served as ammunition for the mob. I immediately ordered a lathi charge to disperse the crowd and with the meagre force we were able to drive the crowd back to some distance. However, by this time, the crowd had swelled to over 5000 and had started pelting stones on the police from all sides. As we were outnumbered and the situation was getting out of control, I ordered firing of tear smoke grenades and cartridges. However, to our bad luck, the wind turned against us and the tear smoke came back into our faces resulting in the police themselves having to retreat. This emboldened the mob. They started pelting stones on the police with renewed vigour resulting in several policemen getting injured. I, too, sustained an injury on my hand from a stone hit. Seeing that the situation was going out of control and as a last resort after warning the crowd that we would open fire, I ordered firing of five rounds. Those days our Armed Police were provided with .303 rifles. These are lethal weapons and a person hit with a bullet from these rifles would either be killed or suffer a grievous injury depending on where he was hit. As soon as we opened fire, we saw a few persons falling and the mob immediately dispersed. We found three persons lying on the ground, who had been hit by the bullets. Unfortunately, all of them were young boys and all were dead. As so often happens in such cases, the main culprits skulk away after starting the trouble and the innocent ones suffer. In any case, the firing had the desired result as the situation was brought under control and the train was allowed to proceed on its journey to Miraj.

After everything was over and the situation brought under control, the District Magistrate came to the Railway Station and said that we should have waited a little longer for him to come before taking action. I told him that the situation could not wait for his arrival as I had waited long enough and I had no idea when he would come as he had failed to come earlier in spite of several messages sent to him including his own Tahsildar informing him about the gravity of the situation. It was a clear case of dereliction of duty on his part and avoiding taking responsibility but as usual these officers are able to get away with it as no action was taken against him in spite of my report and clear evidence of his failure to do his duty.

After attending to the formalities at Harihar which had come back to normal by about 1 p.m., I left for Davangere, where I heard that as a result of the events at Harihar, some miscreants were starting to create trouble. By the time I reached Davangere at about 2 p.m., a mob of about 2000 had already gathered around the Davangere Extension Police Station and the nearby Inspection Bungalow. As such I was met with a hostile reception when I arrived there. Here at least the local Asst. Commissioner, who was also the Sub-Divisional Magistrate, was present in the Police Station. After explaining what had happened at Harihar, we were all in the Police Station planning our strategy to deal with the situation. I had already sent a wireless message to Police Hqrs. in Bangalore giving an account of what had happened at Harihar and requested for reinforcements to be sent as the situation in Davangere was explosive. There was a huge maidan in front of the PS in which the crowd was gathered and by about 3 p.m. it had swelled to over 5000. The crowd was becoming increasingly violent and had started shouting slogans against the police. At the nearby I.B., where my car was parked, they smashed all the glasses of the car and set it on fire about which I was informed. As there was nothing I could do about it, I refused to be provoked. Davangere Ext. PS is a two-storey building. We, that is the SDM, the local DSP and other junior officers and myself were standing on the balcony surveying the crowd below and discussing on how to deal with the situation. Suddenly, at about 4 p.m., the mob started pelting stones at us from below, narrowly missing us but one stone just missed the SDM and hit the wall behind. He immediately panicked and shouted "fire, fire, fire". Two armed constables, who were on the balcony with us, immediately opened 4 rounds of fire. The mob immediately dispersed.

However, as a result of the firing, one young man, who was later identified as a student in one of the local colleges, was hit by a bullet and killed. With this, the situation was immediately brought under control. Though it remained tense that entire evening and night, re-enforcements of police from nearby Police Stations were brought to Davangere, where regular patrolling was organised to ensure that there were no more incidents of violence.

The Range DIG, whose Hqrs. was in Bangalore, arrived in Davangere only around 11 p.m. by which time the situation was fully under control, though very tense. He had brought with him a platoon of Karnataka State Reserve Police, which were immediately deployed at strategic points and also utilised for patrolling.

A Magisterial Enquiry was ordered into the police firing at Harihar and Davangere, though there was a demand for a judicial inquiry. The enquiry reports fully justified the firing and action taken by the police. The then Chief Minister of the state, who was himself from Chitradurga district and who knew the relatives of some of the boys killed in the police firing, had come to Davangere to ascertain for himself what had happened and was satisfied that the action taken by me was fully justified as he never once said anything critical about it. On the other hand, my own Inspector General of Police, who had not even cared to visit the place and ascertain the facts for himself, was somewhat critical about opening of fire, as the senior officers never liked any police firing in their jurisdiction, which could embarrass them with the Government.

This incident took place very early in my career and fortunately was the only one in which I had to order opening of fire by the police resulting in the death of three persons. It was indeed a traumatic experience both for me and my wife, whom the mob tried to attack in the I.B., where she was staying and had to be protected by one of the local Sub-Inspectors and the IB staff. I also lost my private car in the violence and although the insurance company refused to compensate me for it, the Chief Minister was magnanimous enough to issue a Special Government Order granting me compensation for the entire amount for which the car had been insured. The then Chief Minister was the late Shri Nijalingappa, a just and fair person, who respected and supported officers, whom he considered were honest and doing their duty. I was only sorry that our own senior officers were not as understanding and supportive.

In conclusion, I would like to say that though the experience was a very traumatic one, I felt satisfied that as a very young and junior officer, I was able to handle a very difficult and sensitive situation effectively and brought it under control very promptly, though unfortunately at the cost of a few lives, which was unavoidable. We see more serious situations these days, where our officers are hesitant to act, probably looking for instructions from above and where no one is prepared to take responsibility. I would only exhort young police officers of today that they should first and foremost do their duty as per law and the Constitution they have sworn to defend. If they do so, they would not only satisfy their own conscience but earn the respect and regard of the public without which they cannot function effectively.

16

Flag Hoisting at Idgah Maidan, Hubli, Karnataka State—Origin of the Problem

R. RAMALINGAM

The Idgah Maidan at Hubli is a prayer ground situated centrally and surrounded by houses and shops on all sides. Hubli city is the political centre of Northern Karnataka and a communally sensitive place. A long standing dispute regarding the status of Idgah Maidan and whether a shopping complex could be constructed there, is pending in the courts of law.

The state unit of the BJP declared that it would hoist the National Flag at the Idgah Maidan on the eve of the Republic Day in 1992. This was vehemently opposed by a registered society which had been claiming possession of the open ground and also the right to construct a shopping complex. Government of Karnataka decided not to allow flag-hoisting in the Maidan as it would result in communal tension and breach of peace. There were minor incidents of violence during the Republic Day 1992 and many people were arrested. Flag-hoisting in the Maidan was successfully prevented by the police.

Developments over the Years

The BJP declared that it would again hoist the flag on the Independence Day in August, 1992. A similar situation developed, with the same consequences. The Government declared that hoisting of the National Flag in the disputed Maidan would result in communal violence in the sensitive city of Hubli. At this time around, the BJP was able to mobilise more support and there was more violence during Independence Day 1992.

During the year 1993, the Republic Day and Independence Day were celebrated under curfew. Police enforced total curfew for three days in the city. The objective of the curfew was to prevent flag-hoisting in the Maidan. The police were of the view that flag-hoisting could be prevented and law and order maintained by imposing a total curfew. A similar situation of curfew continued during Republic Day 1994. The people of Hubli were affected badly and lived in darkness during National holidays. There was no meeting point. The issue developed into a serious problem and created suspicion among the communities. Even small incidents resulted in violence. An uneasy atmosphere prevailed in Hubli.

Serious Violence during Independence Day 1994

Under these circumstances, during Independence Day 1994, senior BJP leaders announced their intention of participating in the flag-hoisting. There was palpable tension developing as the Independence Day approached. The police mobilised a huge force and also declared that curfew would be imposed again. Agitators declared that they would violate prohibitory orders and hoist the National Flag at Idgah Maidan. There was tension on the eve of the Independence Day. On the morning of the Independence Day, a group of people came out of their houses, shouted slogans and marched towards Idgah Maidan, violating the prohibitory orders. The police, who were under orders to prevent flag-hoisting, used force to disperse the mob. Finally, the police opened fire and five persons died in the firing. The situation was brought under control and the government ordered a judicial enquiry.

Political Change

In the ensuing elections in November 1994, the Janata Dal came to power. The new government wanted to solve the problem amicably. The police department suggested that Anjuman

Islam, an organisation, claiming possession over Idgah Maidan, could hoist the flag on Republic Day without cases pending in court. It was an uphill task to convince the Anjuman Islam and minority community leaders to agree to this suggestion. The Government took political steps and convinced the minority leaders and Anjuman Islam to hoist the National Flag at Idgah Maidan on the Republic Day 1995.

The Government directed the DGP to personally supervise the security arrangements on Republic Day.

Police Approach and Security Arrangements

During the last few years the local police were convinced that flag-hoisting in the Maidan should be prevented for maintaining peace. However, they were not able to convince the local people as to why National Flag could not be hoisted. The situation deteriorated year after year. The police were enforcing curfew rigorously. People had to spend National holidays under curfew. Police started dreading these days and forced to remain indoors fearing the worst.

For the Republic Day 1995, the police decided not to enforce curfew. Though some sections of the police were apprehensive, the decision was widely welcomed by the press and the public.

Another serious friction developed between the organisers, Anjuman Islam, and the police. The leaders wanted the flagpost in an extreme corner of the Maidan. It would not be befitting to the flag on the occasion but the organisers were adamant. Ultimately, the police agreed. Overnight, the police decorated the place with a shamiana and flower pots without shifting the flagpost. The decorations and shamiana created an illusion of a prominent place for the flagpost. People could see the flag-hoisting without really understanding where the flagpole was.

At the appointed time on 26 January, 1995, the organisers, VIPs and press persons were allowed to enter the Maidan. No unauthorised persons were allowed near the Maidan. The flag-hoisting took place in a dignified manner and the National Anthem was sung with great fervour. The audience witnessed a historic occasion and the dignity of the National Flag was maintained. The surging crowds outside the Maidan were kept at a distance by the police and the flag-hoisting ended peacefully. Later, leaders of different political parties were permitted inside the Maidan to witness the National Flag flying with all its dignity.

The entire state celebrated the event. The Government received commendations from all sides. The minorities were also happy. Peace was maintained in the city and the newspapers praised the police arrangements.

Thus, a potentially explosive situation was handled with great care and tact by the Government and the police. An irritant was successfully removed.

The success of the strategy shows the need for the police to be proactive in solving issues instead of taking action after breach of peace occurs.

17

Indian Politics and the Scales of Justice

E. RAMMOHAN

I had worked as Superintendent of Police, Khasi Hills, Shillong, from February 1976 to July 1979, and then joined the Central Bureau of Investigation at Shillong as Superintendent of Police. The city had witnessed some Bengali bashing from mid-1978 to mid-1979 with young Khasi ruffians beating up Bengalis in isolated parts of the town. Some strict policing with foot patrols in civil dress had caught some of these ruffians and by mid-1979, the incidents petered out. Meanwhile, the foreigners agitation had started in Assam, and its effect was felt in all the Northeastern states, particularly Shillong, the capital city of Meghalaya, as there was a Bengali population of one lakh in the town concentrated around the Jail road and Umpling. In one of the bandhs in Shillong in 1978, called by the Khasi Students Union, the youth of the two communities, Kahsis and Bengalis, had almost come to blows in Umpling before the situation could be defused. The Durga Puja celebration in Shillong passed off peacefully in October 1979, without much tension. During the Kali Puja, serious trouble broke out, when a procession carrying a Kali idol was attacked by a group of Khasis. The immediate cause could not be established, but it was rumoured that Bengali boys in the procession made some offensive remarks about the Khasis. If this was not true, the incident could have been premeditated. From this first incident, the situation spiralled out of control because of a weak administration not willing to take strong action. For instance, on one occasion, a procession of Bengalis coming from Laban to the Deputy Commissioner's office, was shouting slogans against the Khasis, when they were spontaneously attacked by office peons and subordinate staff from the Secretariat. In the first instance, there was no one to tell the Bengalis not to make provocative slogans. In the second instance, the Deputy Commissioner was present along with the Superintendent of Police and a platoon of C.R.P.F. at the spot, but did not give the order to the C.R.P.F. to lathi-charge and disperse the unlawful assembly.

I had gone to Imphal in December for supervision of cases there, when I heard of serious communal trouble in Shillong. When I reached Guwahati on 22 December, I was told at Burnihat on the way up to Shillong that there was mayhem and murder at Shillong and curfew had been enforced and the Army called out. I reached Shillong at about 21.00 hours and found the city in darkness and Army patrolling the streets. I went to the Police Station and found the Chief Secretary and the Inspector General of Police and all the Secretaries there. I was told that there was a serious incident near Lailyngkot village, where several Bengalis had been killed. In the town too, ten Bengalis were killed. The next day, I could find out the facts of the case. On 22 December, in the morning, a bus had left Dawki, a town on the Bangladesh border, for Shillong, not knowing that curfew was going to be imposed in Shillong on that day. The bus takes about three hours to reach Shillong from Dawki. At Upper Shillong, the bus stopped to pick up two Punjabi sweepers from the Air Force. When the bus reached Fifth Mile, a crowd of Khasi boys led by a local tough, stopped the bus, asked the Khasi passengers to get down. There were five Bengalis who had got in at Dawki. The Khasi boys did not allow them to get down. The bus was then forced to reverse and piloted by two boys on a motorcycle, forced to drive back, followed by the rest of the gang of Khasi boys in a jeep, belonging to the leader of the group. Before following the bus, the boys picked up pieces of firewood from a jeep taxi. The two Punjabi sweepers also remained in the bus. Short of Lailyngkot, on the way to Pynursla, is a bridge over a small mountain stream. The motorcycle, piloting the bus, stopped in the middle of this bridge, forcing the bus to stop. The gang of boys following the bus surrounded it and dragged the five Bengalis from the bus down to the bed of the stream and then beat them to death with the firewood pieces. Some of the boys, who did not have firewood picked up pieces of rock from the hillside and hit the hapless Bengalis repeatedly with the rocks. When their blood lust was satiated, the boys got back in the jeep and forced the driver of the bus to drive it down to Shillong. They warned the conductor, the driver and the two Punjabi sweepers not to speak to any one about the incident, threatening them that if they dared to tell the police they would meet the same fate as the Bengalis.

I had been Superintendent of Police, Shillong for three and a half years and I had several good sources in the town. I had got the account of what had happened from one of my good sources, but the either would not tell me or probably did not know whose bus was involved. Meanwhile, the Governor Shri L.P. Singh called me and asked me if the C.B.I. could take over the case. I informed him that the C.B.I. had some excellent investigating officers (I.O.) at Delhi and I had also a very good Inspector at Shillong, but the State Government had to give a requisition to the Centre and consent was to be obtained under the Delhi Special Police Establishment Act before the C.B.I. could take over the investigation. The next day, I learnt that the C.B.I. was only to assist in the investigation. A team of two scientists from the Central Forensic Laboratory (C.F.S.L.) was also arriving the next day to assist. The Inspector and I had a detailed discussion with the I.O. of the case. The first direction I gave was to have blood samples taken from the deceased and sealed and kept. Surprisingly, this had not yet been done. The next day, we visited the place of occurrence, along with the two scientists from the C.F.S.L., one of whom was a physics expert, while the other was a serologist. Near Lailyngkot, the outlines of the five hapless Bengalis, who were killed, were etched on the soft green grass in red. The physics expert directed the I.O. to seize samples of the soil from around the outline of the five bodies. He said that if we could arrest the suspects quickly, we might recover traces of soil from the place, from the shoes and trousers folds of the suspects. The serologist suggested that there were bound to be bloodstains on the shirts and trousers of the accused. Soil samples were seized by the I.O. as suggested. Meanwhile, a source met me and told me that the driver and owner of the bus were utkhars (non-Khasis). After some cajoling he told me the owner's name. I sent word to him confidentially. The next morning he came. It was deep winter in Shillong and the morning temperature was –3 degrees. When the utkhar owner of the bus came, I found him sweating profusely. Sweat was dripping down to the floor of the verandah. He promptly admitted that the bus in question was his and the driver was also an uthkar like him. He said if the murderers found out that he had spoken to the police, he and his driver would be killed. After a good deal of persuasion their statements were recorded. Meanwhile, my C.B.I. Inspector and the I.O. managed to get information from a couple of sources that the boys involved were from a notorious village at Fifth mile and the gang was led by a young man from the village. He had also managed to get the names of several boys, who were part of the group, who had killed the five Bengalis, and the name of the leader. The police raided the village and managed to arrest most of the boys involved in the incident. The police also recovered blood spattered trousers and shirts, and mud encrusted shoes from the houses of the suspects. Obviously, the killers had absconded from their houses after hiding the blood stained clothes, thinking that the police might raid their houses the next day. Their absconding actually gave them away. The leader at first would not tell where his jeep was, but after some interrogation he led the police to a nullah in the village where he had hidden it. The hood of the jeep had smudged blood stained fingerprints, where the killers had ridden back from the place of occurrence standing on the rear bumper holding on to the top of the jeep. All the seized blood spattered trousers, shirts, mud encrusted shoes and the bloodstained hood were laid out in the police station before the physics expert and the serologist from the C.F.S.L. The physics expert said he would be able to match with the soil from the soles of the shoes, while the serologist said that the blood from the stains on the clothes were enough to match with the seized blood samples from the deceased. I, particularly, asked him about this and he reiterated his views.

On the basis of source information and the statements of the three eyewitnesses, the driver of the bus and the two sweepers, a Test Identification Parade (T.I.P) was arranged in the court of the Additional District Magistrate, since he had jurisdiction in the tribal areas. The conductor of the bus had stated that he could not identify any of the accused. The remaining three had said they could identify the accused. On the day of T.I.P., conducted in the jail, an unruly crowd of supporters of the killers was allowed to intimidate the witnesses. The conclusion was forgone. None of the three eyewitnesses identified any of the suspects. The police had to rely on scientific evidence alone to prosecute the accused.

A month later, I was recalled as the Superintendent of Police of the Khasi Hills district. I now directly supervised the case. By end February, we had finished the investigation. There was very little to be done, as there was no hope of any one turning approver. I had decided to send the forensic samples to the C.F.S.L. for their expert opinion. The I.O. after sealing the samples before the Magistrate took the parcel to Delhi personally. He returned and reported that the scientists of the C.F.S.L. were pleased with the way the samples were packed and labelled.

Two months went by. One day the I.O. of the case came to me and sought a confidential meeting. He told me that a source of his from the Fifth mile village had come to the Police Station and informed him that the leader of the group, who had killed the five Bengalis, had gone to Delhi to square up the case. He had returned and was entertaining some friends in one of the sleazy hotels in Bara Bazaar, Shillong, shouting in a drunken state that he had met Sanjay Gandhi in Delhi and promised to set up the Youth Congress in Shillong. Sanjay Gandhi had agreed. The C.F.S.L. had been directed to give its opinion that the blood samples sent could not be identified as human blood. With this the case was bound to be closed. I was naturally shocked to hear this and immediately went to the Inspector General of Police and informed him of this and asked him to request the Director, C.F.S.L. to see that the opinion was honestly given. The Inspector General said that the C.F.S.L. would not do any thing so bad. Two weeks later, the opinion of the C.F.S.L. came, stating that the blood from the splattered clothes could not be identified as human blood. The physics expert had opined that the mud samples from the shoes of the suspects tallied in chemical composition with the samples of mud recovered from the site of the murder. On the strength of this we chargesheeted the case. Barely two weeks after this, the leader of the group, the main accused of our case, was made the Youth Congress President of Shillong. Of the five Bengalis killed, two of them happened to be the father-in-law and the husband of a young lecturer in a local college. The other three were the husbands and fathers of wives and children. Who was to recompense them ? They were to be denied even a feeling that justice would be done to the killers of their husbands and fathers. Who was going to assuage the pain in their hearts ? Certainly not the callous politicians of this country.

18

Many a Man Who Failed Actually Never Tried

S.K. SHARMA

Overnight transfers and even suspension of senior police officers at the whims and fancy of the powers that be seem to have become a routine matter these days. Frequent press reports on the subject no more attract public attention nor sympathy for these public servants. Reading these disturbing news items day in and day out, my thoughts went back to my own days in the police service in Rajasthan and on deputation at the Centre. I wondered how in those days we could effectively deal with sensitive situations and defy extraneous pressures without getting mauled in the process. My own experiences flashed back and in all humility I am putting some of them down for posterity.

Preventing Jodhpur Communal Riots

Jodhpur city had witnessed very serious communal riots in the 1970s and since then it has been marked as communally sensitive. During my posting as DIG of Police, Jodhpur Range in the early nineteen eighties, an ugly incident between members of two communities created serious communal tension. Utmost efforts were being made by the police and the magistracy with the help of some influential members of both communities to prevent communal violence. The situation seemed to be gradually coming under control when, to our surprise, certain elements of one community started adopting difficult postures which would thwart all efforts made towards securing a rapprochement. The district machinery again went into top gear to bring the warring factions to the table and geared up the preventive measures simultaneously. However, this time the reconciliatory moves were proving ineffective because of hard posturing by one community leaders and the retaliatory attitudes of the other.

It was then that the DM and the SP met me and what they revealed was startling. A state cabinet minister, known for his strong communal leanings and not too savoury a criminal past was in town and had brought about the change in an otherwise improving situation. The two officers strongly felt that while outwardly the minister was making reconciliatory gestures, they had confirmed information that he was inciting one vociferous faction against the other community. They were of the view that if this continued any longer, the situation would be ripe for a full-scale communal riot in the city and adjoining areas. From experience we knew that any effort to prevent the minister from playing with communal fire would only create more problems. A unanimous view that emerged was that the best way to prevent his interference would be to somehow get him out of the district on some pretext.

On the assurance of the DM and the SP that the administration would be able to diffuse the situation, once the incitement and machinations of the minister stopped, I took the responsibility to try and get the minister out of the district. I realized that this could be achieved only by prevailing on the Chief Minister (CM) to ask the concerned minister to get back to Jaipur forthwith for whatever reasons. Now generally such an unorthodox request to the CM should be routed through the Director General of Police, who in turn may involve the Home Secretary (HS) or Chief Secretary (CS) or take the Intelligence Branch route. These officers often have their own ideas about handling the situation which may be at variance with our local perception. Any way, the situation was too explosive to brook any delay inherent in a hierarchical approach. What was paramount in my mind was the need to prevent bloodshed and loss of innocent lives and property which was bound to occur if the situation was allowed to drift.

In Rajasthan, the post of Divisional Commissioner had been abolished since long and was revived in 1986, Range DIG of Police was, therefore, the only officer responsible for coordination of law and order matters at the division level. Making bold to bypass hierarchies, I rang up the CM's office in Jaipur directly only to be told that he was away to Delhi for a meeting. Pressing on I was able to locate him in Delhi and managed to establish contact with his Secretary, an IAS officer. Just as well because the Secretary happened to be a very perceptive and mature officer apart from being very helpful. He understood the situation immediately and even mentioned its implications for the state government. He assured me that he would convey my views to the CM forthwith and would revert back to me quickly with whatever decision CM took.

In the interregnum, I developed cold feet and my own approach appeared to me to be somewhat quixotic. What if the CM found my request to withdraw a minister from the district unpalatable and viewed it as a sign of incompetence on our part to squarely deal with the situation. Could I expect support from the bypassed hierarchies if my strategy backfired as I had the temerity to approach the CM directly ? No, I must think positive. I have known these officers as very magnanimous personalities who were always supportive of the field officers. Even the CM would appreciate my initiative and would like to avoid use of force by the police if the only cost is to get the minister out of the district on some pretext. But what would be the reaction of the minister towards me when ultimately he comes to know the truth of my getting him out of the district?

I was jolted out of my broodings by the telephone buzz. The Secretary to CM was on the line within ten minutes of my call. What he said was music to my ears. The CM had talked to the minister and he would be heading for Jaipur 'sooner than later'. After informing the DM and the SP of this development, the first thing I did was to apprise the DGP and HS of the action taken by the CM at our behest and casually slipped in an apology for not having consulted them before hand due to time constraint. As J.F. Kennedy said, "Success has many parents but failure is an orphan." Both officers were highly appreciative of the initiative taken at the 'local' level. In fact, one of them said that as soon he came to know about the presence of the minister in Jodhpur in the current situation he had thought of getting him out somehow.

At about 10 that night, I got a call from Jaipur by the minister informing me that he had had to hurriedly leave Jodhpur 'for an urgent work' in Jaipur and therefore could not meet me. On behalf of the state government he exhorted that the district administration should take all necessary action to maintain peace in the city and offered his fullest help and cooperation. On my part, I showed utmost respect to him and assured him that no effort would be spared to carry out his instructions and that with his 'cooperation' normalcy shall be restored in the city at the earliest. And that is exactly what the district administration did in about three days' time, thereby preventing a calamitous situation of bloodshed and destruction.

Chaliay, Theek Hai (OK, It's All Right)

I was posted as DIG, Bikaner Range, on my reversion to the state cadre after 13 long years of deputation to BSF and other (non-police) government organisations at the Centre. I was almost relearning the police work and told my District Superintendents jocularly that I had placed myself on six months probation to pick up the lost threads. What I left unsaid was that I wished to learn the management of environment in which the police worked and which had undergone a sea change in the years I was out of the state.

I learnt my first lesson soon enough. Within a few days of my joining, the Minister of State for Home (SHM) called me up to say that an inquiry against a Sub Inspector of Police had been conducted and that I should ensure that stern action was taken against him. Next day, I received a message from the Minister's office that the aforesaid SI should be placed under suspension.

I obtained the file from the office and studied it very carefully. However, I could not find anything in the inquiry report nor in the comments of the concerned senior officers which could warrant any departmental action, leave alone stern action, as desired by the minister. I even thought of reopening the inquiry lest the earlier inquiry was not conducted impartially. Meanwhile, I happened to speak to some police officers and came to know that this SI, having obliged a political faction initially, strongly resisted their pressures beyond a point. Hence the complaint against him. I dropped the idea of a fresh inquiry keeping it as a last resort if the pressure persisted.

In a couple of days, I got a call from the SHM again. This time he asked me somewhat aggressively if the SI had been placed under suspension. I sensed he meant business. In a split second I decided to be equally business like because otherwise the matter would become difficult to handle. Instead of humming and hawing or trying to stall the issue, I told him 'politely but firmly' that what to talk of suspension there was no material on record to award even a minor penalty to the SI. I hastened to add that I had therefore closed the proceedings on merits accordingly. I expected a rude if not a violent reaction but was surprised to hear "Oh Achha? Chaliye, Theek Hai" (Oh is it? OK, its all right). This could mean anything. I did feel uneasy for a couple of days. There could be repercussions, I thought. But if there were any, at least I am not aware of them. All I know is that I completed my tenure of two years at Bikaner from where I was posted to a bigger and politically hotter Range.

Shown the Door

I had been posted as Chief Vigilance Officer in the India Tourism Development Corporation (ITDC), a public sector company, on deputation, more or less of my own choice, after completing my tenure with Shah Commission of Inquiry. In ITDC, I tried to evolve a new concept of 'Commercial Vigilance' qualitatively different from the anti-corruption model in the government. This implied, *inter alia*, a cost effective approach to prevent corrupt practices through appropriate proactive measures, sensitizing the Unit Heads about corruption and motivating them to act as vigilance officers themselves in their own interest. The Vigilance Department could then concentrate on vital areas and assist the company to take highly deterrent and exemplary action so as to create an environment of high level probity and curb the venality and malpractices which affected the productivity and profitability of the company.

Duty Free Shops (DFS), run by the company at all international airports in the country, were one such area that came under the vigilance scanner because of generally odious reputation of leakage of duty free goods from the airports and sale of spurious stuff at the DFS. Sustained vigilance led to the recovery of eight Scotch Whisky bottles from the possession of a DFS employee just outside the airport terminal building by the vigilance staff. Incisive investigations brought out concrete documentary evidence of misappropriation of these bottles (not of money—which had already been paid to avoid detection). Two employees were eventually dismissed. In another case, Seiko watches sold at the DFS were found to be spurious.

Further probing into the affairs of DFS brought into sharp focus one particular employee who appeared to be the fountainhead of corruption and unethical practices in this area. In fact, he was quite open and brash about his corrupt practices for reasons which came to light later as the noose came closer to his neck. His TA bills showed that he travelled by air and claimed train fare as per his entitlement. He could not be faulted on that but the question was how could he afford it. When confronted with this, he made a startling disclosure that he even stayed in Five Star hotels during official tours wherever ITDC hotels did not exist. At least one such stay was verified. Incidentally, he also possessed an imported car which he used for coming to office, again something which *per se* cannot be taken exception to. This may have made our vigilance staff envious of him, at least momentarily, but actually it strengthened their resolve to fully probe all aspects, and if there was evidence of his venality, to make an example of this case for deterring others.

A further probe brought glaring evidence of irregularities and improprieties in the documents of purchases, etc. It appeared that invoices were either fake or entries therein had been doctored. The purchases involved in these documents amounted to thousands of US Dollars. The in-depth investigation into the working of DFS, coupled with dismissal of two DFS employees for smuggling eight liquor bottles out of an airport, appeared to have somewhat rattled the nonchalant employee.

At about this time, a major event took place in the country. The Janata Dal Government failed to complete its tenure and the Congress came back to power. That was when I realized the extent of this employee's prowess, reach and extent of influence that lay at the back of his brashness and dare devilry. The rumours had it that the employee was very close to the ruling party bosses. True enough, as I started receiving calls from high and influential quarters asking me not to meddle with DFS and stop harassing this particular employee. Even an IPS officer in CBI, who somehow maintained contact with the Central Ministers or at least with their Private Secretaries, alerted me through a common friend that I was headed for a disaster, if I pursued the matter.

Perhaps this employee and I shared a common personality trait—nonchalance for the consequences. I did, however, take a cue from the advice-cum-warnings conveyed to me by influential quarters and speeded up the investigations before the matter got stalled and the file summoned etc. The in-house probe gave clear indications of commission of cognizable offences of misappropriation, forgery and fraud. A full-fledged investigation under criminal law would bring out a lot more. A detailed investigation report was put up to C & MD for approval to refer the case to CBI for investigations (had kept the concerned DIG CBI informed of the developments throughout).

Around this time a highly disturbing development took place for me personally. I was told by the CMD to give in writing that I was no longer interested in serving in the ITDC and should therefore be reverted to my State cadre. The provocation for this was cited to me to be the Congress Government's allergy to my past association with the Shah Commission of Inquiry. However, I could not help linking this move with my active role in inquiries relating to the well-connected DFS employees.

Be that as it may, I refused to put in my papers on the dictated lines and asked what if I did not oblige. I was told that in that case perhaps my office could be inspected to condemn and then sack me from the ITDC. This threat looked to be real after the CMD told me that he had already put in his papers (he had been appointed to ITDC by the Janata Dal Government). Though generally very amenable to the advice of my seniors. I strongly felt that the suggested course of action was a slimy and ignominious way of quitting and considered it below the dignity of an IPS officer to chicken out under such pressures. I could not therefore persuade myself to follow the official 'advice' and decided to take on the 'inspection' or any other similar gimmick concocted for showing me the door. My appetite for novel experiences (after all that was what impelled me to join the ITDC) dictated that facing such pressure tactics would be an experience worth its while. However, nothing of the sort happened and I stayed on albeit for a while only. But the ITDC lost an excellent CMD.

The new CMD saw the case after a while and felt it reeked of corruption and wondered why such a man had not been suspended so far. He asked me if he could suspend the employee before referring the matter to the CBI. In all fairness, I apprised him of the quarters from where I had received calls in this case and said that there could be many more such calls to him if drastic action like suspension was taken. I said this not only as a matter of duty towards a new CMD but also to gauge his much talked of boldness. I am glad to record here that the new CMD proved equal to his reputation and shot back 'if you have withstood pressure, so can I' or words to that effect.

Orders for suspension of the employee were issued and the case was referred to the CBI for further investigation. I learnt that cases were registered at different points of time, one for disproportionate assets, one for fraudulent deals and another under Excise Act after preliminary inquiries. CBI raids were conducted on the premises of not only the delinquent employee but also of some cargo and clearance agents, among others. Recoveries from the residence of the employee made startling revelations. There were blank invoices of some foreign suppliers of duty free goods purporting to be signed by the authorised agents of the supplier companies (this explained the suspicious nature of the invoices detected during vigilance inquiries). Also found in his house were ownership documents of a two and a half-storied residential house in a well-known locality of South Delhi and sizable quantity of duty free liquor, among other things.

The CBI investigations came to a stage where it became necessary for an investigating officer to go to Hong Kong for collection of crucial evidence to prove certain offences including import of spurious watches. I learnt that while the concerned branch of the CBI was keen to marshal evidence available in Hong Kong, the concerned Joint Director (later he was Director CBI) had ruled out any such move. I personally tried to impress upon him the importance of this investigation but he refused to be persuaded. The reason cited to me was 'shortage of staff'.

Things started to look up for the vigilance with the new CMD after a while. Firstly, he was an appointee of the new government and highly influential. Secondly, he was very pro-vigilance and favoured expansion of the existing token vigilance set up and its operations. Though initially very cold to me, we gradually started getting along very well. However, if I thought that the move to oust me from ITDC had fizzled out due to my firm attitude or otherwise I was sadly mistaken. It had merely been postponed. On the 5th January 1981, I received a letter from the Ministry of Tourism directing me to hand over charge at the ITDC and report to the Ministry of Home Affairs in the forenoon of 6th January 1981 on completion of my two years tenure. In the absence of CMD, who was on tour, I consulted the Company Secretary and asked to be relieved without any further delay as per the directions of the

Ministry. Having failed to contact the CMD, he agreed to take over charge from me since the Ministry's letter left no choice in the matter.

Thus came to an end my two years tryst with ITDC, full of rich and varied experiences and a sense of satisfaction of having worked in a commercial environment. The CMD returned from his tour the next day, ahead of schedule. He feigned annoyance with me for not having waited for him before handing over charge. When I remonstrated that the Ministry's letter gave me no choice, he then let it out that it was just as well that I handed over charge as nothing could have been done. Later I learnt that the CMD had cut short his tour on hearing about this development and met the powers—that—be. But so great was the provocation for getting me out of the ITDC that even an influential officer like him could not have any say in the matter.

Was it Shah Commission or my role in the DFGS case or both that led to this situation is not known to me till today. Nor was I much concerned about it as an IPS officer and was happy to go back to my State cadre and to my profession of active policing after 13 long years. After all, I had completed my initial tenure with ITDC and it was perfectly legitimate for the Ministry not to extend my stay for genuine or extraneous reasons and despite a strong request by the CMD to the contrary.

As for the CBI cases against the DFS employee, I learnt that subsequent to my leaving the ITDC all of them fizzled out one by one. The disproportionate assets case was reportedly dropped in face of the evidence produced by the accused of having taken loans from friends and relatives for the excess assets. In the other case, the CBI is reported to have recommended major penalty action against two DFS employees and 'suitable' action against another. Though I do not exactly know, the Excise Act case may have similarly fizzled out in the court. The very fact that the DFS employee was regularly promoted in due course indicates that nothing was done by way of departmental action against him as recommended by the CBI in one case.

The last episode (ITDC) was in fact the first in point of time among the three episodes narrated above. While it saddened my heart to leave the ITDC abruptly and virtually unceremoniously, it did not dampen my resolve to continue to work with zeal and without fear or favour. This is amply evident from the other two experiences depicted here and which came in quick succession of my ITDC experience. The uniqueness of the ITDC experience (and of working in Shah Commission of Inquiry) was the lesson learnt that sincere and hard work though bliss by itself may not always be rewarding and may demand a heavy price by way of opprobrium it attracts sometimes.

I have no pretensions that there were any extraordinary attributes in officers of earlier times except high moral values, integrity and self-respect that pervaded the environment at the time. I have the highest admiration for the present day officers who are at the helm of affairs. The professional challenges and extraneous pressure, they are facing, are much more onerous and complex, both qualitatively and quantitatively. Unfortunately for them, the environment in which they are placed is highly vitiated in terms of values, standards and dignity. The standard of integrity has, therefore, touched its nadir all over.

It is said about 'advice' that those who are wise do not need it and those who are unwise do not heed it. I would, therefore, not venture to give any advice and conclude by quoting John Wooden:

"Don't let what you cannot do interfere with what you can do."

19

Caste Barrier

SANKAR SEN

It was a warm and sultry evening at Rourkela, where I was posted as the Range D.I.G. I was about to leave for the club to see a movie when a phone call came from Cuttack. It was the voice of the Inspector-General of Police. He told me that a devastating tornado had hit some villages in the neighbouring district of Keonjhar, causing heavy destruction of human lives and property. He wanted me to immediately rush to Keonjhar (a distance of nearly 150 miles from my Range Headquarters) to mobilise the police personnel and organise relief and rescue operations for the tornado-affected villages.

Hurriedly packing a bag, I left for Keonjhar within an hour. The journey was nightmarish. The winding ghat roads of the sub-division were in a bad state of disrepair and because of the rains, they were slushy and slippery. The beautiful, dark and deep forests on either side of the road looked grim and menacing in the darkness of the night. The wind howled and roared. Incessant rains spattered on the windscreen of the car, reducing visibility almost to nil. By God's grace, I reached Keonjhar at midnight, safe and sound. I found that several officers of the district, including the S.P. and the District Magistrate, had already left for the tornado-hit villages. The officers present at the district headquarters were unaware of the extent of the devastation and loss of human lives caused by this massive calamity. All kinds of exaggerated rumours were afloat.

Early next morning, I reached the scene of devastation, which was at a distance of nearly 30 miles from the district headquarters. It was a traumatic experience. About eleven villages had been razed to the ground as if a giant bulldozer had rolled over them. Trees had been uprooted, electric poles twisted and broken, and houses, both mud and mortar-built, had just disappeared. The havoc caused by the elemental fury of nature was to be seen to be believed. Dead bodies of human beings and carcasses of animals were lying scattered. The villagers were dumbfounded and almost stupefied by the suddenness and magnitude of the calamity. Their eyes were dry. They had no more tears to shed. All they could do was to look at us with vacant and listless eyes, not knowing what to do. Groups of relief workers were moving about, but they too were at a loss and did not know how to go about their job.

The first task of the police officers and men was to arrange for the cremation of the dead bodies lying near the ruins of the broken houses. The putrid smell of the dead bodies was filling the air and deepening the sense of death and gloom all around. I advised my officers to seek help of the villagers for the disposal of the dead bodies. But I was amazed to find that even in this hour of grim tragedy, when the devastating fury of nature had levelled down all distinctions between the high and the low, the rich and the poor, there was a distinct reluctance on the part of many of the villagers to lift the dead bodies and place them on the funeral pyres arranged by us. Because of their reluctance, this work had to be done by the police officers.

When I asked some of the passive onlookers the reasons for their unexpected reluctance to step forward and help in the cremation of the dead bodies of their compatriots, they replied that they belonged to the upper Mahanta caste and hence, could not, and would not, bury the dead bodies, as they had found out that some of them belonged to lower sub-castes. To me, this was a shocking revelation. Even this massive natural calamity, which had uprooted trees, demolished houses and reduced everything to the ground, could not break the villagers' age-old caste prejudices and inhibitions, which had a vice-like grip on their minds.

20

Remembering J.C. Ghose

SANKAR SEN

I still vividly remember my first meeting with him. It was sometime in March, 1962, when I was posted in Cuttack for training as the probationary A.S.P., along with a batchmate of mine. One of our first calls of duty was to call on the Inspector-General of Police in his office. Both of us, in full ceremonial dress, and perspiring profusely out of nervousness and trepidation, marched into his room. Mr. J.C. Ghose, I.G.P., was poring over some files. A heavy, middle-aged man with an impassive face and a grim look, he raised his eyes from the files and had a close look at us, leaving us almost frozen. For the next ten minutes, he did not utter a word and the two of us remained petrified in our chairs. I could, however, see that despite this forbidding silence, there was a kindly and humorous twinkle in his eyes. After this phase of silence, he made some queries about our training and then asked us to go and meet the other senior officers of his office. We scampered out of his room, a little dazed and unsure of the impression the I.G.P. had formed about the two blundering A.S.Ps.

After a few months, my friend and batchmate, Mr. P.K. Mishra, got married. Mishra's marriage took place at his native place; but he arranged after a few days, a tea party at the bungalow, which we were both sharing at that time. The invitees were mostly the senior officers of the Service. Many of the senior officers did not care to turn up; some came late and unblushingly offered some trite excuses. But the senior-most officer of the cadre, Mr. J.C. Ghose, along with his wife, came exactly in time and showed by his example that the marriage ceremony of an A.S.P. is an important social function, which other senior officers should make it a point to attend in time.

Many other incidents and episodes associated with Mr. Ghose flash before my mind's eye. I never worked under him as one of his staff officers, but had the opportunity of coming in contact with him while I was posted at Cuttack. Behind his frosty and forbidding exterior and apparent unapproachability, there was a soft, tender and even warm heart. I have never seen him speaking disparagingly or pejoratively about others, including those who had not exactly been fair to him. Like Newman's True Gentleman, he had too much good sense to remember injuries and nurture grudges against others. Will Durant has defined a gentleman as "one who is perpetually considerate". One cannot imagine Mr. Ghose as anything except kindly and considerate-qualities which are mistakenly considered as unpolice-like. Many of his contemporaries thought and felt that just as Brasidas, the noblest of Spartans (as any student of Greek history knows), was a Spartan by mistake, J.C. Ghose was perhaps a police officer by mistake.

Once, he visited, with some of his friends, a place near Cuttack called Charbatia, where I was posted as the Commandant of an O.M.P. Battalion. He was, at that time, functioning as the Transport Controller. One of his acquaintances, who was also known to me, requested for a police tent to be used in a picnic they had planned to organise in a nearby field. There were difficulties in acceding to this request and so I kept mum. In the evening, I got a phone call from Mr. J.C. Ghose from Cuttack. He felt that perhaps I was hesitating to give a negative reply to his friends in his presence and advised me not to comply with the request as the police tentage cannot be given for the use of private individuals.

Mr. Ghose was always fair and upright. I had a feeling that he was, at times, slow in taking decisions, because he wanted to be scrupulously fair and just. He had all the makings of an excellent judge.

A senior civil servant is expected to be honest, but Mr. Ghose's standard of integrity was one of the highest that I have ever seen. There could not be even a whisper against his character and conduct. He set almost exemplary standards of propriety and incorruptibility before his subordinates; and by his personal conduct, typified the maxim, 'Noblesse Oblige'—rank imposes obligations. I have seen him in some of his moments of both agony and ecstasy. He was never off balance and always retained his dignity and quiescence.

Times are changing. The values of the old world that we saw when we entered the service are crumbling and being supplanted by altogether new concepts and perceptions. J.C. Ghose was a typical representative of the old world and carried with him the aura and grace of that era. After retirement, he went to Calcutta, where he breathed his last. When I communicated the news of his death to a colleague of mine, he just said, "Here comes the end of another good man". In this cruel and self-seeking world, the number of truly good and civilised human beings is not many. The death of such a man will bring silent tears to the eyes of many who knew and admired him. The saying of Socrates just before his death comes to one's mind:

"Think this certain that to a good man no evil can happen in life or death". J.C. Ghose was a good man!

Index